W9-DFJ-889

Official Rules of Chess

Second Edition

794.1
mor

Official Rules of Chess

Second Edition

Edited By

Martin E. Morrison

USCF Executive Director
Chairman, USCF Tournament Direction Committee
Chairman, FIDE Rules Commission

*

UNITED STATES CHESS FEDERATION (USCF) SECTION

Official 1977 Edition

William B. Abbott   *Stephan C. Gerzadowicz*
Joseph W. Lux   *John M. Osness*
of the USCF Tournament Direction Committee
Collaborators

WORLD CHESS FEDERATION (FIDE) SECTION

Official FIDE Publication
Authorized 1977 English Edition

Harry Golombek   *A. Kiprov*
Philip G. Haley   *Paul Klein*
Armin Heintze   *Ole Schøller-Larsen*
of the FIDE Rules Commission
Collaborators

This edition supersedes the preceding (1974) edition
and becomes effective January 1, 1978.

David McKay Company, Inc.   38808

NEW YORK ROSLYN HIGH SCHOOL LIBRARY
Roslyn Heights, New York

To H. J. J. Slavekoorde (1907–1977), who retired in 1976 as Chairman of the FIDE Rules Commission, having served in that capacity since 1969, in recognition of his substantial contributions to the work of the Commission and the first edition of the *Official Rules of Chess.*

OFFICIAL RULES OF CHESS

FIRST EDITION
Copyright © 1975 by United States Chess Federation

SECOND EDITION
Copyright © 1978 by United States Chess Federation

All rights reserved, including the right to reproduce this book, or parts thereof, in any form, except for the inclusion of brief quotations in a review.

PRINTING HISTORY

First Edition, June 1975

Second Corrected Printing, November 1975

Second Edition, February 1978

Second Corrected Printing, March 1979

Library of Congress Cataloging in Publication Data
Main entry under title:

Official rules of chess.

Includes index.
CONTENTS: Abbott, W. B. et al. United States Chess Federation section: official 1977 edition.—Golombek, H. et al. World Chess Federation (FIDE) section: official FIDE publication, authorized English edition, 1977.
1. Chess—Rules. I. Morrison, Martin E. II. United States Chess Federation. III. World Chess Federation.
GV1457.033 1977   794.1   77-20237
ISBN 0-679-13053-5
ISBN 0-679-14043-3 pbk.

Manufactured in the United States of America

10 9 8 7 6 5 4 3 2

Contents

FIDE SECTION

Preface to the FIDE Section

Laws of Chess
Including
FIDE Interpretations of the Laws of Chess
And
Tournament Rules of the
United States Chess Federation

Rules for
Five-Minute Lightning Chess

GENS UNA SUMUS

Preface to the FIDE Section

This section contains the Laws of Chess of the World Chess Federation (commonly known as FIDE, the acronym of its original name in French, *Fédération Internationale des Échecs*). Included with the Laws are the FIDE Interpretations, which have the same validity as the Laws themselves. This book contains the only authorized English text of the FIDE Laws and Interpretations.

The FIDE material in this section is current through the FIDE Congress of 1977. To keep the material in this section current, a supplement containing any changes in the Laws or Interpretations will be issued by the publisher in odd-numbered years, and a revised edition, in even-numbered years. This book and any supplements issued will be available from the U.S. Chess Federation, 186 Rt. 9W, New Windsor, N.Y. 12550, U.S.A., and the World Chess Federation, Passeerdersgracht 32, Amsterdam-Centrum, Netherlands.

As the authorized English edition is being published in the United States, the United States Chess Federation has published its own supplementary Tournament Rules together with the FIDE Laws and Interpretations in a different typeface. These rules are the sole responsibility of the USCF and do not conflict with, but supplement, the FIDE Laws and Interpretations. Each article of the Laws is followed by its Interpretations (if any) and then by its supplementary USCF Tournament Rules (if any). To facilitate reference, each Law, Interpretation, and Tournament Rule has been given its own reference code.

Any comments on the contents of this book may be addressed to the editor, Martin E. Morrison, at the U.S. Chess Federation, who will be happy to reply to them.

Laws of Chess
Including FIDE Interpretations of the Laws of Chess and Tournament Rules of the United States Chess Federation

Part I. General Laws

ARTICLE 1 · INTRODUCTION

The game of chess is played between two opponents by moving pieces on a square board called a "chessboard."

FIDE INTERPRETATION ART. 1 (1959). GENERAL OBSER-VATIONS. The Laws of Chess cannot, and should not, regulate all possible situations that may arise during a game, nor can they regulate all questions of organization. In most cases not precisely regulated by an Article of the Laws, one should be able to reach a correct judgment by applying analogously stipulations for situations of a similar character. As to the arbiters' tasks, in most cases one must presuppose that arbiters have the competence, sound judgment, and absolute objectivity necessary. A rule too detailed would deprive the arbiter of his freedom of judgment and might prevent him from finding the solution dictated by fairness and compatible with the circumstances of a particular case, since one cannot foresee every possibility.

The decisions of the Commission* are founded on the above general principles.

FIDE INTERPRETATION ART. 1 (1974). During recent years the Commission has been more or less overwhelmed by a

---

* The FIDE Rules Commission, which proposes Interpretations of the Laws.

steadily growing number of proposals and questions. That, of itself, is a good thing.

However, there is a marked tendency in those many questions and proposals to bring more and more refinements and details into the Laws. Clearly the intention is to get more and more detailed instruction concerning "how to act in such and such a case." This may be profitable for a certain type of arbiter, but at the same time may be a severe handicap for another, generally the best, type of arbiter.

The Commission in its entirety takes the firm position that the Laws should be as short and as clear as possible. The Commission strongly believes that minor details should be left to the discretion of the arbiter. Each arbiter should have the opportunity, in case of a conflict, to take into account *all* the factors of the case and should not be bound by too detailed sub-rules which may not be applicable to the case in question. According to the Commission, the Laws of Chess must be short and clear and leave sufficient scope for the arbiter to deal with exceptional or unusual cases.

The Commission appeals to all chess federations to accept this view, which is in the interest of the hundreds of thousands of chess players, as well as of the arbiters, generally speaking. If any chess federation wants to introduce more detailed rules, it is perfectly free to do so, provided—

(a) they do not in any way conflict with the official FIDE Laws;

(b) they are limited to the territory of the federation in question; and

(c) they are not valid for any FIDE tournament played in the territory of the federation in question.

USCF TOURNAMENT RULES ART. 1 (1–4). GENERAL TOURNAMENT REGULATIONS.

USCF TOURNAMENT RULE ART. 1 (1). *The organization sponsoring the tournament must be a USCF affiliate. The organization sponsoring the tournament may appoint a local committee to take charge of the arrangements and has the fol-*

lowing powers and duties: to appoint the tournament director; to make advance arrangements for the tournament, including playing quarters and any equipment to be supplied; to establish the date and time of each session; to establish the conditions of entry; and to be generally responsible for the observance of all USCF procedures and policies.

USCF TOURNAMENT RULE ART. 1 (2). *All games must be played in the tournament rooms on the days and at the times specified by the tournament organizers, unless the director makes or accepts other arrangements (e.g., a first-round game may be arranged to be played in advance of the start of a tournament).*

USCF TOURNAMENT RULE ART. 1 (3). *For the inclusive dates of his play, each player in the tournament must be a USCF member in good standing.*

USCF TOURNAMENT RULE ART. 1 (4). *Play shall be governed by the Laws, by the FIDE Interpretations of the Laws, by the USCF Tournament Rules and Pairing Rules, and by all USCF procedures and policies.*

ARTICLE 2 · THE CHESSBOARD AND ITS ARRANGEMENT

2.1. The chessboard is composed of 64 equal squares alternately light (the "white" squares) and dark (the "black" squares).

2.2. The chessboard is placed between the players in such a way that the corner square to the right of each player is white.

2.3. The eight rows of squares running from the edge of the chessboard nearest one player to that nearest the other player are called "files."

2.4. The eight rows of squares running from one edge of the chessboard to the other at right angles to the files are called "ranks."

2.5. The rows of squares of the same color, touching corner to corner, are called "diagonals."

ARTICLE 3 · THE PIECES AND THEIR ARRANGEMENT

3.1. At the beginning of the game, one player has 16 light-colored pieces (the "white" pieces), the other has 16 dark-colored pieces (the "black" pieces).

3.2. These pieces are as follows:

A white king	usually indicated by the symbol		♔
A white queen	" " " " "		♕
Two white rooks	" " " " "		♖
Two white bishops	" " " " "		♗
Two white knights	" " " " "		♘
Eight white pawns	" " " " "		♙

A black king	usually indicated by the symbol		♚
A black queen	" " " " "		♛
Two black rooks	" " " " "		♜
Two black bishops	" " " " "		♝
Two black knights	" " " " "		♞
Eight black pawns	" " " " "		♟

3.3. The initial position of the pieces on the chessboard is as follows:

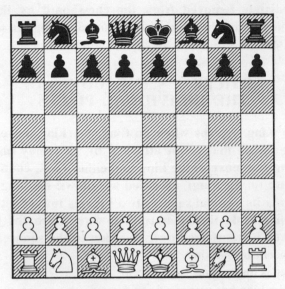

ARTICLE 4 · THE CONDUCT OF
THE GAME

4.1. The two players must alternate in making one move at a time. The player with the white pieces commences the game.

4.2. A player is said to "have the move" when it is his turn to play.

ARTICLE 5 · THE GENERAL
DEFINITION OF THE MOVE

5.1. With the exception of castling (Article 6.1), a move is the transfer of a piece from one square to another square which is either vacant or occupied by an enemy piece.

5.2. No piece except the rook, when castling, and the knight (Article 6.5) may cross a square occupied by another piece.

5.3. A piece played to a square occupied by an enemy piece captures it as part of the same move. The captured piece must be immediately removed from the chessboard by the player making the capture. See Article 6.6b for capturing "en passant."

ARTICLE 6 · THE MOVES OF
THE INDIVIDUAL PIECES

6.1. The King. Except when castling, the king moves to any adjoining square that is not attacked by an enemy piece.

Castling is a move of the king and either rook, counting as a single move (of the king), executed as follows: the king is transferred, from its original square, two squares toward either rook on the same rank; then that rook toward which the king has been moved is transferred over the king to the square immediately adjacent to the king.

Castling is impossible—

(a) if the king has already been moved, or

(b) with a rook that has already been moved.

Castling is prevented for the time being—

(a) if the king's original square or the square which the king must cross or that which it is to occupy is attacked by an enemy piece, or

(b) if there is any piece between the king and the rook toward which the king is to be moved.

FIDE INTERPRETATION ART. 6.1 (1971). If a player in castling starts by touching the rook, he should receive a warning from the arbiter, but the castling shall be considered valid.

If a player, intending to castle, touches king and rook at the same time and it then appears that castling is illegal, the player has to move his king. If the king has no legal move, the fault has no consequences.

FIDE INTERPRETATION ART. 6.1 (1974). The Commission regards the warning by the arbiter an adequate means of dealing with those who castle in the wrong manner.

The Commission disagrees with the principle that if the king has no legal move, then a move with the rook shall be made, which would apply if the move was initially one with the rook alone.

FIDE INTERPRETATION ART. 6.1 (1975). Question: If a player moves his king two squares, intending to castle with the king's rook, and it then appears that castling is illegal, can the player castle on the other side (provided, of course, that castling on that side is legal)?

Answer: The answer is yes. The player has to make any legal move he chooses with his king, from its original square. There is no reason why that legal move should not be castling on the queen's side.

6.2. The Queen. The queen moves to any square (except as limited by Article 5.2) on the file, rank, or diagonals on which it stands.

6.3. The Rook. The rook moves to any square (except as limited by Article 5.2) on the file or rank on which it stands.

6.4. The Bishop. The bishop moves to any square (except as limited by Article 5.2) on the diagonals on which it stands.

6.5. The Knight. The knight's move is composed of two different steps; first, it makes one step of one single square along the rank or file and then, still moving away from the square of departure, one step of one single square on a diagonal.

6.6. The Pawn. The pawn may move only forward.

(a) Except when making a capture, it advances from its original square either one or two vacant squares along the file on which it is placed, and on subsequent moves it advances one vacant square along the file. When capturing, it advances one square along either of the diagonals on which it stands.

(b) A pawn attacking a square crossed by an enemy pawn which has been advanced two squares in one move from its original square may capture this enemy pawn as though the latter had been moved only one square. This capture may be made only on the move immediately following such an advance and is called capturing "en passant."

(c) On reaching the last rank, a pawn must be immediately exchanged, as part of the same move, for a queen, a rook, a bishop, or a knight of the same color as the pawn, at the player's choice and without taking into account the other pieces still remaining on the chessboard. This exchanging of a pawn is called "promotion" and the action of the promoted piece is immediate.

FIDE INTERPRETATION ART. 6.6c (1971A). In a game between Player A (White) and Player B (Black), B played on the 45th move . . . c1. However, he neglected to exchange the pawn immediately for a queen. On his scoresheet he had written 45 . . . c1Q and stopped his clock afterwards. Then he left the board. At the time, his opponent was not present. When A returned to the board, he protested because B had not immediately exchanged the pawn on c1, though B told him the piece on c1 was a queen. The arbiter decided as follows: A's clock was restored to the position it had before the move . . . c1 was made. B had to make his move 45 . . . c1Q again, as it was obvious that he intended to promote that pawn to a queen. Then the game was resumed in the normal way.

The Commission confirms the decision of the arbiter.

FIDE INTERPRETATION ART. 6.6c (1971B). In a competition, if a new piece is not immediately available, the player must ask for the assistance of the arbiter before making his move. If this request is made and there is any appreciable delay in obtaining the new piece, the arbiter must stop both clocks until the required piece is given to the player having the move. If no request is made and the player makes his move and stops his clock without exchanging the promoted pawn for a new piece, he is breaking the Laws and must be given a warning or a disciplinary penalty, such as the advancement of the time on his clock. In any case, the opponent's clock must be set back to the time it registered immediately before the player stopped his clock, the position on the chessboard must be reestablished to what it was before the player moved his pawn, and the clock of the player having the move must be started.

The player must then make his move correctly, in the manner specified in Article 6.6c.

FIDE INTERPRETATION ART. 6.6c (1973). The penalty referred to in FIDE Interpretation Art. 6.6c (1971B) is meant to be indefinite. The penalty should depend on the circumstances.

ARTICLE 7 · THE COMPLETION OF THE MOVE

A move is completed—

1. in the case of the transfer of a piece to a vacant square, when the player's hand has released the piece;

2. in the case of a capture, when the captured piece has been removed from the chessboard and the player, having placed on its new square his own piece, has released the latter from his hand;

3. in the case of castling, when the player's hand has released the rook on the square crossed by the king; when the player has released the king from his hand, the move is not yet completed, but the player no longer has the right to make any other move than castling; or

4. in the case of the promotion of a pawn, when the pawn has been removed from the chessboard and the player's hand has released the new piece after placing it on the promotion square; if the player has released from his hand the pawn that has reached the promotion square, the move is not yet completed, but the player no longer has the right to play the pawn to another square.

ARTICLE 8 · THE TOUCHED PIECE

8.1. Provided that he first warns his opponent, the player whose turn it is to move may adjust one or more pieces on their squares.

FIDE INTERPRETATION ART. 8.1 (1974). A player who wishes to adjust one or more pieces when his opponent is absent may make the adjustment after warning the arbiter of his intention.

USCF TOURNAMENT RULE ART. 8.1 (1). *If a player wishes to adjust pieces on their squares when his opponent is absent and a director is not available, he may ask a spectator or a player who is not on the move to witness the adjustment. It is only the player whose turn it is to move who may adjust pieces on their squares. If the other player adjusts his own or his opponent's pieces, he may be penalized at the discretion of the director.*

8.2. Except for the above case, if the player having the move touches—

(a) one or more pieces of the same color, he must move or capture the first piece touched that can be moved or captured; or

(b) one of his own pieces and one of his opponent's pieces, he must capture his opponent's piece with his own piece; or, if this is not possible, move his own piece; or, if even this is not possible, capture his opponent's piece.

FIDE INTERPRETATION ART. 8.2 (1972). In a recent game the player with the white pieces claimed that his opponent violated Article 8.2 by touching a piece, then moving a different piece. Black denied the accusation, and an arbiter was called to the board. There was no independent witness of any kind to the alleged violation, so the arbiter rejected the claim for lack of evidence.

The Commission declares that the arbiter was correct. As in the case of all other Laws, unbiased evidence is required to support any claim by a player that his opponent violated a Law. If the accused player denies the allegation and it is impossible to prove otherwise by the testimony of an arbiter or other disinterested witness, it is just a question of one player's word against that of his opponent. An unsubstantiated claim would have to be rejected.

FIDE INTERPRETATION ART. 8.2 (1974A). A player who touches more pieces than those indicated in this Article may be penalized at the discretion of the arbiter.

FIDE INTERPRETATION ART. 8.2 (1974B). Question: If a player reaching for a piece to make a move (but not having touched it yet) touches another piece with his arm in passing, is this grounds for the opponent to claim that the player must move that piece?

Answer: A piece is considered to be touched under this Article only when a player touches it with the intention of making a move with it. Doubtful cases are left to the discretion of the arbiter.

FIDE INTERPRETATION ART. 8.2b (1975). Question: White has a pawn on c5 and a queen on c4, and Black has a rook on d6. White intends to play cxd6. Many players are used to touching first the piece to be captured and, with the same hand, at (nearly) the same time, the capturing piece. In this example White touches the black rook, and in the following fraction of a second, he reconsiders his intended move and touches the white queen. According to Article 8.2b he can play any move he likes with the queen, and the fact that he touched the black rook does not count any more. The Article gives priority to a move with the player's own piece over the capture of an opponent's piece. In most cases, would it not better correspond to the original intention of the player to give priority to the capture?

Answer: The Commission declines to give an Interpretation on the basis of hypothetical cases alone. It should be remarked, however, that the seemingly "obvious" solution (changing the order of possibilities in Article 8.2b) is no good, because in that case another hypothetical case could be constructed, in which the reverse could happen.

8.3. If the move or capture is not possible, the player is free to make any legal move he chooses.
8.4. If a player wishes to claim a violation of this rule, he must do so before he touches a piece himself.

FIDE INTERPRETATION ART. 8.4 (1974). The enforcement of this Article by the arbiter does not require a claim to be made.

USCF TOURNAMENT RULE ART. 8.4 (1). *The following exception to normal procedure applies only to large tournaments in which it is impossible to supervise play in all games: infringements of Article 8 must be claimed by the opponent unless a director witnesses a violation.*

ARTICLE 9 · ILLEGAL POSITIONS

9.1. If, during a game, it is found that an illegal move was made, the position shall be reinstated to what it was before the illegal move was made. The game shall then continue by applying the rules of Article 8 to the move replacing the illegal move. If the position cannot be reinstated, the game shall be annulled and a new game played.

FIDE INTERPRETATION ART. 9.1 (1963). Question: How are the words "during a game" to be interpreted if a game has been submitted for adjudication? Specifically, is the game considered to be still in progress for the purposes of Article 9.1 if, before the arbiter has registered the result of the game after adjudication, it is established that an illegal move was made or that one or more pieces were accidentally displaced and incorrectly replaced?

Answer: The Commission declares that in such cases a game submitted for adjudication is considered to be still in progress for the purposes of Article 9.1.

USCF TOURNAMENT RULE ART. 9.1 (1). *If the director rules that no time is available to complete a game which must be reinstated or replayed under Article 9, he may take whatever action he deems appropriate.*

9.2. If, during a game, one or more pieces have been accidentally displaced and incorrectly replaced, the position shall be reinstated to what it was before the displacement took place, and the game shall be continued. If the position cannot be reinstated, the game shall be annulled and a new game played.

9.3. If, after an adjournment, the position is incorrectly set up, the position as it was on adjournment must be set up again and the game continued.

9.4. If, during a game, it is found that the initial position of the men was incorrect, the game shall be annulled and a new game played.

FIDE INTERPRETATION ART. 9.4 (1958). Question: What is the procedure when it is established in the course of a game that the game began with colors reversed?

Answer: The Commission declares that this is a situation of the kind indicated in Article 9.4.

FIDE INTERPRETATION ART. 9.4 (1960). In a Swiss-System tournament, the arbiter made a mistake by giving to Player X the white pieces and to Player Y the black pieces instead of the opposite. After detecting the mistake some days later, Player Y claimed that the game should be annulled and a new game played in its stead, with Player Y having the white pieces.

The Commission declares that in accordance with the fundamental principles of Articles 9.4 and 9.5, the claim, since it was submitted after the end of the game, must be rejected.

FIDE INTERPRETATION ART. 9.4 (1973). The Commission states that in the case of FIDE Interpretation Art. 9.4 (1958) it does not matter who made the mistake (even if it was the arbiter as well as both players). The rules must be obeyed in any case.

9.5. If, during a game, it is found that the board has been wrongly placed, the position reached shall be transferred to a board correctly placed and the game continued.

FIDE INTERPRETATION ART. 9.5 (1973). This Article applies only in the case where the initial position of the pieces on the chessboard accorded with that specified in Article 3.3 except that each of the squares on which the pieces rested was of the opposite color. Otherwise, Article 9.4 applies.

ARTICLE 10 · CHECK

10.1. The king is in check when the square it occupies is attacked by an enemy piece; in this case the latter is said to be "checking the king."
10.2. Check must be parried by the move immediately following. If the check cannot be parried, it is said to be "mate." (See Article 11.1.)
10.3. A piece blocking a check to the king of its own color can itself give check to the enemy king.

ARTICLE 11 · THE WON GAME

11.1. The game is won by the player who has mated his opponent's king.

FIDE INTERPRETATION ART. 11.1 (1976). Question:

(1) Player A makes a move that gives stalemate. This move is so menacing (e.g., a threatened mate in one) that his opponent, Player B, resigns. It is subsequently noticed, either by the player or by a spectator or the arbiter, that the last move was a stalemating move. What is the result?

(2) Is the situation affected in any way by the nature of the person who points out the stalemate? For example, if it is a spectator who points it out, is the result of the game any different?

(3) If Player A gives checkmate without realizing it and

then Player A resigns, possibly after one move or more has been made, and afterwards it is pointed out or noticed by Player A that mate was given, what is the result of the game?

(4) Is this situation affected by who points out the mate?

Answer: The Commission reiterates the principle that what happens in consequence of an action or of an omission after the termination of a game is without importance. A checkmating or stalemating move ends the game regardless of subsequent actions or omissions.

Spectators are not to speak or otherwise to interfere in the games. However, if a spectator points out an irregularity, the arbiter may initiate action on his own, but should severely warn the spectator against future interference or even expel him from the tournament room.

11.2. The game is won by the player whose opponent declares he resigns.

FIDE INTERPRETATION ART. 11.2 (1971). If a player shakes hands with his opponent, this is not to be considered as equal to resigning the game as meant in Article 11.2.

ARTICLE 12 · THE DRAWN GAME

The game is drawn—

1. when the king of the player whose turn it is to move is not in check and the player cannot make any legal move. The king is then said to be "stalemated."

2. by agreement between the two players.

3. upon a claim by one of the players when the same position (a) is about to appear or (b) has appeared, for the third time, the same player having the move each time. The position is considered the same if pieces of the same kind and color occupy the same squares and if the possible moves of all the pieces are the same.

The right to claim the draw belongs exclusively to the player—

(a) who is in a position to play a move leading to such a repetition of the position, if he first declares his intention of making this move, or

FIDE INTERPRETATION ART. 12.3a (1960). If the claim turns out to be incorrect (Article 18.2) and the game continues, the player who has indicated a move according to (a) is obliged to execute this move on the chessboard.

FIDE INTERPRETATION ART. 12.3a (1974). A requirement to the effect that a player should not only declare his intention of making a move leading to the repetition of the position but also execute the declared move on the board is not necessary. It is clear that the player who claims the draw has to make the intended move in any case, but the Commission is of the opinion that the declared move should not be immediately executed on the board.

(b) whose turn it is to reply to a move that has produced the repeated position.

If a player executes a move without having claimed a draw in the manner prescribed in (a) and (b), he loses the right to claim a draw; this right is restored to him, however, if the same position appears again, the same player having the move.

FIDE INTERPRETATION ART. 12.3 (1964). Concerning the repetition of a position on the chessboard, a position should not always be considered the same if pieces of the same kind and of the same color occupy the same squares (static identity), but only on the additional condition that the possibilities for moving these pieces are also the same (that is to say, that there is also dynamic identity). If one adds this last stipulation, a player would thus no longer be entitled to demand a draw if, after the repetition of a position, the right to castle or to take a pawn "en passant" had been lost.

4. when a player having the move demonstrates that at least fifty consecutive moves have been made by each side without the capture of any piece or the movement of any pawn.

This number of fifty moves can be increased for certain positions, provided that this increase in number and these positions have been clearly established before the commencement of the game.

FIDE INTERPRETATION ART. 12.4 (1958A). Question: Can a player lose the game by exceeding the time-limit when the position is such that no mate is possible, whatever continuation the players may employ (this concerns Part II of the Laws)?

Answer: The Commission declares that the Laws must be interpreted in such a way that in this case, as in the case of perpetual check, a draw cannot be decreed against the will of one of the players before the situation foreseen in Article 12.4 is attained.

FIDE INTERPRETATION ART. 12.4 (1958B). The Commission declares that this Article concerns only the possibility of indicating in the regulations for a certain tournament or match certain positions for which the number of fifty moves may be increased.

FIDE should not assume the responsibility for inserting into the Laws details which might be revealed as incorrect as a result of future investigations.

Part II. Supplementary Laws
for Competitions

ARTICLE 13 · THE RECORDING
OF GAMES

13.1. In the course of play each player is required to record the game (his own moves and those of his opponent), move after move, as clearly and legibly as possible, on the scoresheet prescribed for the competition.

FIDE INTERPRETATION ART. 13.1 (1970). Question: A player, referring to the Laws, asked his opponent to make his move first and only then to write it down on his scoresheet. It is thought not to be correct to write down the move first and only then to make it on the board. The arbiter of the tournament in question judged the case to be insignificant.

Answer: The Commission is of the opinion that every player who has the move has the choice.

FIDE INTERPRETATION ART. 13.1 (1973). In a tournament game, a player who was not short of time (his opponent was, though) recorded his moves two at a time (one move for White, one move for Black), as was his habit. Several players have the same habit. The arbiter told him that he should record his moves one after another. The player considered this to be an unnecessary disturbance and an indirect help for his opponent, who was in time-trouble.

The question is: is it a breach of Article 13.1 if the moves are not recorded separately, but in pairs (White and Black together), if the player concerned is not in time-trouble?

Answer: Technically speaking, this is indeed a breach of Article 13.1. However, the arbiter should intervene only when the arrears in scorekeeping are more than one move for White and one move for Black.

USCF Tournament Rule Art. 13.1 (1). *Each player is required to record the moves of the game in the manner specified in Article 13.1 on the scoresheet provided or approved by the tournament organizers. Either the algebraic system, recommended by FIDE, or the descriptive system of notation may be used.*

USCF Tournament Rule Art. 13.1 (2). *Except as provided in Supplement No. 4 of the Laws of Chess and the following paragraph, no person may act as the deputy of a player in recording moves.*

If a player's handicap prevents him from recording the moves, moving the pieces on the board, or operating his clock, the director may permit a deputy to perform such duties as the case may require if the player requests a deputy before the game. If the handicapped player is permitted to use a deputy, the opponent must be permitted to use one also.

In general, the tournament director may use his discretionary powers to accommodate the rules to the special needs of a handicapped player. However, he must inform each opponent of the handicapped player, before the start of the game, of any accommodations of the rules he has granted and must ensure that such accommodations do not confer any undue advantage on the handicapped player with respect to his opponent, who must be granted similar accommodations if he requests them.

USCF Tournament Rule Art. 13.1 (3). *When a game is completed, the result must immediately be registered officially with the director or his designee. The manner in which the official registration is accomplished (by signed scoresheets, entering the result on a pairing sheet, etc.) is at the director's discretion.*

USCF Tournament Rule Art. 13.1 (4). *The following exception to normal procedure applies only to large tournaments in which it is impossible to supervise play in all games: infringements of the Laws on Recording of Games (Article 13) must be claimed by the opponent unless the director witnesses a violation.*

13.2. If, extremely pressed for time, a player is obviously unable to meet the requirements of Article 13.1, he should nevertheless endeavor to indicate on his scoresheet the number of moves made. As soon as his time-trouble is over, he must immediately complete his record of the game by filling in the moves omitted from his scoresheet. However, he will not have the right to claim, on the grounds of Articles 12.3 or 12.4, a draw based on any moves which were not written down in accordance with the prescriptions of Article 13.1.

FIDE INTERPRETATION ART. 13.2 (1958). Question: How should the words "extremely pressed for time" be interpreted?

Answer: The Commission, referring back to what has been stated in the General Observations (FIDE Interpretation Art. 1 [1959]), is of the opinion that in each particular case the interpretation should devolve on the arbiter of the competition.

FIDE INTERPRETATION ART. 13.2 (1959). The words "extremely pressed for time" figuring in Article 13.2 cannot be precisely defined. It is the arbiter's task to find out, considering time, the number of moves, and the character of the position at the moment, if these words apply to a player's situation. In this case the arbiter's opinion decides.

If the arbiter thinks the above words do not apply, but if the player refuses to record the game according to Article 13.1, then Article 17.4 should be applied.

If the player does not refuse to comply with the arbiter's request, but declares that he cannot complete his scoresheet without consulting his opponent's, the request for this scoresheet must be made to the arbiter, who will determine whether the scoresheet can be completed before the time-control without inconveniencing the other player. The latter cannot refuse his scoresheet for two reasons: the scoresheet belongs to the organizers of the tournament and the reconstitution of the game will be made on his opponent's time. In all other cases the scoresheets can be completed only after the time-control. At this point two situations may prevail—

(a) if one player alone has not completed his scoresheet, he will do so on his own time; or

(b) if both players have not completed their scoresheets, their clocks will be stopped until the two scoresheets are completed, if necessary with the help of a chessboard under the control of the arbiter, who will beforehand have noted the position.

If in case (a) the arbiter sees that the complete scoresheet cannot help in reconstituting the game, he will act as in case (b).

FIDE INTERPRETATION ART. 13.2 (1967). During the course of a game the two players, under extreme time-pressure, did not write down their moves after move 30. After a series of moves they agreed that they had played at least 40 moves. Being unable to reconstruct the course of the game without the help of a chessboard, they asked permission of the arbiter to reconstruct the game. The arbiter gave permission, and the reconstruction started. The arbiter stopped the clocks, but during the course of the reconstruction, Black's clock was started by White because Black had started to reflect on the game. At the beginning of the reconstruction, Black disposed of one minute and a half for reflection. During the reconstruction this player exceeded the time-limit, and it was discovered that he had made only 39 moves.

The Commission's opinion, as no other details are available, is that the player with the white pieces won the game. (See also FIDE Interpretation Art. 13.2 [1976].)

FIDE INTERPRETATION ART. 13.2 (1972). Question: Concerning Article 13.2 of the Laws about keeping score, is a player in time-trouble obliged to stop his clock with the same hand with which he keeps score?

Answer: The Laws make no such requirement, whether or not the player is in time-trouble, nor is there any Law that requires a player to stop his clock with the hand he uses to make moves on the board.

FIDE INTERPRETATION ART. 13.2 (1974). If an arbiter stops the clocks for reasons mentioned in FIDE Interpretation

Art. 13.2 (1967), then *only* the arbiter decides when the clocks should be started again.

FIDE INTERPRETATION ART. 13.2 (1976). There being a certain ambiguity in the words "as soon as his time-trouble is over," the Commission agrees that when, by the arbiter's count, the prescribed number of moves has been made by each player, the arbiter will require the players to update their scoresheets at that time, if necessary. However, if neither player is aware that he has completed his prescribed number of moves, the arbiter is allowed to use his discretion as to when he tells the players that they must update their scoresheets.

USCF TOURNAMENT RULE ART. 13.2 (1). *The following exception to normal procedure applies only to large tournaments in which it is impossible to supervise play in all games: Completion of scoresheets after the time-control when a player, extremely pressed for time, has obviously been unable to meet the requirements of Article 13.1, is optional at the discretion of the director.*

ARTICLE 14 · THE USE OF THE CHESS CLOCK

14.1. Each player must make a certain number of moves in a given period of time, these two factors being specified in advance.

USCF TOURNAMENT RULE ART. 14.1 (1). *The duration of the first time-control period must be at least one half hour for each player, and the time-limit of any control period must not be faster than an average of two minutes per move (thirty moves per hour) in a national tournament, otherwise one minute per move (60 moves per hour), except when a time penalty has been imposed under USCF Tournament Rule Art. 20.4 (1). The USCF may make exceptions so that some national tournaments may be played at the faster rate allowed other tournaments. If a faster time-limit than an average of two minutes per move is used in any tournament, it must be announced in advance.*

USCF TOURNAMENT RULE ART. 14.1 (2). *Both players' time is cumulative; i.e., the time a player does not use in one time-control period before he has made the specified number of moves is credited to future time-control periods.*

14.2. Control of each player's time is effected by means of a clock equipped with a special device (usually a "flag") for this purpose.

USCF TOURNAMENT RULE ART. 14.2 (1). *In the absence of an evident defect, the falling of a clock's flag and the time on the clock indicate the moment at which the player's time-control period expires. As the players (and, when possible, the director) should have inspected the clock and its flag for evident defects before and during play, and as one minute has been added to the time-control to compensate for any possible minor defects in the accuracy of the clocks, a claim that a flag has fallen prematurely should be accepted only if there is a clear space between the minute hand and the left side of the hour marker when the flag falls.*

USCF TOURNAMENT RULE ART. 14.2 (2). *If the end of a time-control period will not be marked by a flag fall because of absence of a flag or a defective flag, the time-control period is deemed to have expired when there is a clear space between the clockwise side of the appropriate dial marker and the minute hand.*

When any secondary time-control period is less than one hour, both clocks should be reset by moving them forward one hour less the secondary time-control. If the players are allowed to reset the clocks themselves at the end of each time-control period or when both players have made the specified number of moves in each time-control period, the chief director must specify the exact procedure to be used in a written and also, whenever possible, oral announcement in advance of the first round.

14.3. At the time determined for the start of the game, the clock of the player who has the white pieces is set in motion. In the continuance of the game, each of the players, having made his move, stops his own clock and starts his opponent's clock.

FIDE INTERPRETATION ART. 14.3 (1958). Question: How should this Article be interpreted in a case where Black is absent as well as his opponent?

Answer: The Commission considers that Article 14.3 should be applied in all its rigor.

FIDE INTERPRETATION ART. 14.3 (1967). Question: Is an arbiter entitled to call a player's attention to the player's neglect to stop his clock and/or to the fact that the opponent has made a move and put the clock of the player in motion?

Answer: The opinion of the Commission is that an arbiter must refrain from any action of this kind.

FIDE INTERPRETATION ART. 14.3 (1973). FIDE Interpretation Art. 14.3 (1967) is based on the conviction, which the Commission maintains, that the normal handling of the clock should be done solely by the players. If a player forgets to stop his clock when he has made a move, that is *his* responsibility. The arbiter's function is not to correct the faults or omissions of the players in this respect. Furthermore, a correcting action of the arbiter should not depend on whether he notices these mistakes.

USCF TOURNAMENT RULE ART. 14.3 (1). *The chief director should stipulate at the beginning of the tournament the direction the clocks are to face, and the players should seat themselves so that the clocks are to the right of the players with the black pieces. Mechanical clocks should be set so that each unit will register six o'clock when the first time-control expires, one minute being added to the time-control when the clocks are set to compensate for any possible minor defects in the accuracy of the clocks or their flags. The players (and when possible, the director) should inspect the clock and its flags for evident defects before and during play.*

When the round begins, the clock of each player with the

white pieces is started by his opponent, if the latter is present, or by an official if both players are absent. If White is present and Black is absent, White must immediately start his opponent's clock, but need not make his first move. When Black arrives, he stops his own clock and starts White's clock; White then makes his first move. Although White is not required to do so, he may, after starting Black's clock, make his first move before his opponent arrives.

USCF TOURNAMENT RULE ART. 14.3 (2). *When a clock is not available at the beginning of the round, but is brought or obtained later, the following rules apply.*

(a) If both players are present when the round begins, they start play immediately. If a clock becomes available later, the elapsed time of the round is divided equally between the two players.

(b) If one player is absent when the round begins, he is charged with the elapsed time of the round up to the moment of his arrival. The time from his arrival until a clock becomes available is divided equally between the two players.

(c) If both players are absent when the round begins, the player with the white men is charged with the elapsed time of the round up to the moment of his arrival. If his opponent arrives still later, he is charged with the difference between White's arrival time and his own. White makes his first move when Black arrives, and the time from then until a clock becomes available is divided equally between the two players.

USCF TOURNAMENT RULE ART. 14.3 (2)—VARIATION. *In a tournament with a large number of players, if the director believes that the preceding rule cannot be applied, the following procedure may be substituted. However, written and also, whenever possible, oral announcement must be made in advance of the first round, and the same procedure must be used for all games.*

No player may subtract time from a late opponent without starting a clock. If a clock becomes available after the beginning of the round, the director may require that the elapsed time of the round be divided equally between the two players.

(a) If both players are present when the round begins, they start play immediately.

(b) If one player is absent when the round begins, play starts when the player who is present starts the clock he has brought or obtained. If he has not brought a clock and is unable to obtain one, play does not start until the opponent arrives.

(c) If both players are absent when the round begins, play starts when the first player arrives and starts the clock he has brought or obtained. If he has not brought a clock and is unable to obtain one, play does not start until the opponent arrives.

USCF TOURNAMENT RULE ART. 14.3 (3). *In any game without a clock at the beginning of the round, a player loses by default if he does not arrive within one hour after the time specified for the start of play. If neither player arrives within one hour, the game is lost by both (Article 17.4).*

USCF TOURNAMENT RULE ART. 14.3 (4). *With the exception of any games postponed by consent of the director, all the games of each round must start promptly at the time specified (USCF Tournament Rule Art. 1 [2]). If feasible, the director should give five minutes' warning, then announce that play must begin.*

In a large tournament, if it is impractical for the director to announce the beginning of a round, players should be urged, in advance, to begin their games promptly by starting their opponents' clocks. The players should also be informed that no permission is needed to start games at the specified time if the pairings have been posted.

14.4. When determining whether the prescribed number of moves has been made in the given time, the last move is not considered as completed until after the player has stopped his clock.

FIDE INTERPRETATION ART. 14.4 (1974). The Commission rejects the idea that the flag is considered to have fallen from the moment that the fact is mentioned, since the idea is not entirely correct. The flag is considered to have fallen when the arbiter observes the fact. In cases where no arbiter is present, the flag is considered to have fallen when a claim has been made to that effect by a player.

FIDE INTERPRETATION ART. 14.4 (1976). In formal competitions, Article 14.4 provides that a move is not considered as completed until after the player has stopped his clock, in accordance with Article 7 (this general principle applies whether there is at the board a witness to these actions or not).

In other words, the player's flag must remain unfallen after the opponent's clock has been started. (Exception: Rarely a player's own flag will fall while his opponent's clock is running. This circumstance, if it can be clearly proved, implies an evident defect of the flag.) Only if it can be clearly proved that a checkmate or stalemate had been completed on the board or that a claim of a draw by repetition had been made under Article 12.3, is it of no importance whether or not the player was able to stop his clock before his flag had fallen.

14.5. Every indication given by a clock or its device is considered as conclusive in the absence of evident defects. The player who wishes to claim any such defect must do so as soon as he himself has become aware of it.

FIDE INTERPRETATION ART. 14.5 (1958). Having been asked for more exact definitions as to what constitutes evident defects of a clock, the Commission replies by referring back to the general principles clearly outlined in the General Observations (FIDE Interpretation Art. 1 [1959]).

FIDE INTERPRETATION ART. 14.5 (1971). With regard to Articles 14.5 and 14.6, the arbiter should endeavor to check all clocks periodically to make sure that they are operating properly.

A clock with an obvious defect should be replaced, and the time used by each player up to the moment when the game was interrupted should be indicated on the new clock as accurately as possible.

If one unit of the defective clock has stopped, the corresponding unit of the new clock should be advanced so that the total time indicated by the two units is equal to the time the session of the competition had been in progress.

If both units have stopped, the difference between the total of the times registered by the defective clock and the elapsed time of the session should be divided in half and each unit of the new clock advanced by this amount.

If any of the above clock adjustments would result in an indication that a player had exceeded the time limit, or if the time used by each player cannot be accurately determined, the arbiter may set the hands of the new clock in accordance with his best judgment.

FIDE INTERPRETATION ART. 14.5 (1973). The last paragraph of FIDE Interpretation Art. 14.5 (1971) clearly indicates that the correction of the hands of the clock(s) should not lead to disastrous results for one (or both) of the players. For that very reason, the last paragraph of the Interpretation gives the arbiter the option to use his own judgment.

FIDE INTERPRETATION ART. 14.5 (1974). The Commission is of the opinion that with regard to FIDE Interpretation Art. 14.5 (1973) the players involved should never have the right to deal with the situation of a defective clock. This task belongs exclusively to the arbiter.

USCF TOURNAMENT RULE ART. 14.5 (1). *The following exception to normal procedure applies only to large tournaments in which it is impossible to supervise play in all games: the players are responsible for checking their clocks to see that they are operating properly and must report defects to the director.*

14.6. If the game has to be interrupted for some reason for which neither player is responsible, both clocks shall be stopped until the matter has been adjusted. This should be done, for example, in the case of an illegal position to be corrected, in the case of a defective clock to be exchanged, or if the piece which a player has declared he wishes to exchange for one of his pawns that has reached the last rank is not immediately available.

FIDE INTERPRETATION ART. 14.6 (1972). Question: With regard to Article 14.6, is the sudden illness of a player during the course of a game or the sudden decease of a close relative covered by this Article?

Answer: With regard to Article 14.6, if the sudden illness during the course of a game is deemed to be of a short duration, then the answer is yes, but if it is not regarded as likely to be brief, the answer is no. In this case and also in the case of the sudden decease of a close relative, the matter must be left to the discretion of the arbiter.

USCF TOURNAMENT RULE ART. 14.6 (1). *A player does not have the right to stop both clocks during a game except at adjournment (Article 15.1). However, if a director is not present, a player may stop both clocks while summoning a director in order to claim that a flag has fallen prematurely (USCF Tournament Rule 14.2 [1]) or that a new piece for a promoted pawn is not immediately available. Stopping both clocks at any other time may be done only by a director in accordance with the rules or when he believes it is justifiable. A player who loses time on his clock while summoning a director to present a claim may have that time restored to him at the director's discretion.*

14.7. In the case of Articles 9.1 and 9.2, when it is not possible to determine the time used by each player up to the moment when the irregularity occurred, each player shall be allotted up to that moment a time proportional to that indicated by the clocks when the irregularity was ascertained. For example, after Black's 30th move it is found that an irregularity took place at the 20th move. For these thirty moves the clocks show 90 minutes for White and 60 minutes for Black, so it is assumed that the times used by the two players for the first twenty moves were as follows:

$$\text{White} \quad \frac{90 \times 20}{30} = 60 \text{ minutes}$$

$$\text{Black} \quad \frac{60 \times 20}{30} = 40 \text{ minutes}$$

FIDE INTERPRETATION ART. 14.7 (1975). Question: In a game as part of a team match, both players were short of time as the time-control approached. Both made their moves in time, and the game was then adjourned to allow both clubs to decide what claim to submit to the adjudicator; the rules of the competition stipulated that after the first full session of play, the game should be sent for adjudication rather than continued.

Before either team had submitted an adjudication claim, but two or three days after the match, one player discovered that his opponent had made an illegal 33rd move, the game having been adjourned at the 40th move. Examination of both players' scoresheets confirmed that the move had been illegal.

The arbiter of the competition ruled that since neither club had submitted a claim to the adjudicator at the stage when the illegality had been discovered, the game could not be regarded as completed. He decided, however, that since the game could not be continued without a major distortion of the time situation, the player who had made the illegal move should lose the game. The club concerned appealed against this decision. The appeals committee overruled the earlier decision and ordered the game continued from the stage where the illegality occurred. They further ruled (a) that the player who had made the illegal move should move the piece which he had touched to make the illegal move and (b) that to offset the distraction produced by the resumption of the game, the player who had made the illegal move should be allocated only 5 minutes on his clock, while his opponent should be allocated 24 minutes, in accordance with Article 14.7.

Would the Commission care to comment on the issue raised by this case?

Answer: The decision of the arbiter of the competition (loss of the game for the player who made the illegal move) was wrong. The decision of the appeals committee (to give the right portion of time to the player who did not make the illegal move and to give considerably less time to the player who made the illegal move) was wrong. The formula of Article 14.7 of the Laws should have been applied to both players, not to just one of them. There is no indication whatsoever that the formula of Article 14.7 may be ignored; neither is there any indication in the Laws themselves nor is there any Interpretation to this effect in existence. Leaving alone the reasons of the appeals committee for its decision, it should be remarked that the faulty decision made might easily be seen and felt as a kind of punishment, which should be avoided at all cost.

ARTICLE 15 · THE ADJOURNMENT OF THE GAME

15.1. If a game is not finished upon conclusion of the time prescribed for play, the player having the move must write his move in unambiguous notation on his scoresheet, put this scoresheet and that of his opponent in an envelope, seal the envelope, and then stop the clocks. If the player makes the said move on the chessboard, he must seal this same move on his scoresheet.

FIDE INTERPRETATION ART. 15.1 (1966). In adjourning a game, the player having the move made a note of the adjourning move, placed the paper in an envelope, sealed it, and put it on the table; however, the clocks were not stopped. When the arbiter took the envelope, the player asked him to return it, since he was still thinking over his move. The arbiter refused to do so, stating that in that phase of the game it was not possible to permit modification of an adjourning move.

The Commission declares that an adjourning move had not been definitely made and therefore the decision of the arbiter was not correct.

FIDE INTERPRETATION ART. 15.1 (1973). The Commission declares that it should be left to the discretion of the arbiter whether games should not be adjourned more than an hour before the end of the time fixed for adjourning.

USCF TOURNAMENT RULE ART. 15.1 (1). *At the end of the playing session—*

(a) If, for any reason, it is impossible to determine how many moves have been made in a game that is to be continued or adjourned, it shall proceed from the final position on the board with the move number that begins the new time-control.

(b) If unfinished games are to be adjourned and play resumed at a later time, Article 15 applies. Unless permitted by the director, a game must not be adjourned until the prescribed number of moves has been made by each player and until the time specified for the end of the session.

(c) If unfinished games are to be continued, with or without a brief recess, and the time between rounds is limited, games should be completed as quickly as possible. Provided that prior announcement has been made, secondary time-controls faster than the first time-control may be used if they accord with the requirements of USCF Tournament Rule Art. 14.1 (1).

(d) Permanent adjudications should be used only as a last resort, not as a standard practice in any tournament.

15.2. Upon the envelope shall be indicated—
   (a) the names of the players,
   (b) the position immediately before the sealed move,
   (c) the time used by each player, and
   (d) the name of the player who has sealed the move and the number of that move.

USCF TOURNAMENT RULE ART. 15.2 (1). *The date and time the game is to be resumed should also be indicated on the envelope. Both players should sign the envelope to indicate that they agree with and understand the information it contains.*

15.3. Custody of the envelope must be assured.

ARTICLE 16 · THE RESUMPTION OF THE ADJOURNED GAME

16.1. When the game is resumed, the position immediately before the sealed move shall be set up on the chessboard, and the time used by each player when the game was adjourned shall be indicated on the clocks.

FIDE INTERPRETATION ART. 16.1 (1973A). The Commission accepts, as a recommendation, the proposal that before the last round starts all adjourned games should be finished.

FIDE INTERPRETATION ART. 16.1 (1973B). The Commission declares that it should be left to the discretion of the arbiter whether, in order to finish the adjourned games as quickly as possible, the arbiter has the right, on the day reserved for adjourned games, to interrupt a game of presumed long duration in favor of one or more adjourned games which might be finished more quickly.

FIDE INTERPRETATION ART. 16.1 (1973C). The Commission declares that it should be left to the discretion of the arbiter (provided that in FIDE tournaments no player should be forced to play more than seven hours a day) whether the duration of the time fixed for the playing off of adjourned games may be prolonged, if necessary, but not by more than two hours, provided that the players concerned have been warned in advance.

USCF TOURNAMENT RULE ART. 16.1 (1). *If players agree on the result of an adjourned game before the time specified for its resumption, both players must notify the director (at a reasonable hour) or they may become liable to penalty under Article 17.2.*

USCF TOURNAMENT RULE 16.1 (2). *In all tournaments every effort should be made to complete all unfinished games from previous rounds before the last round begins.*

16.2. The envelope shall be opened only when the player having the move (the player who must reply to the sealed move) is present. That player's clock shall be started after the sealed move has been made on the chessboard.

FIDE INTERPRETATION ART. 16.2 (1974). Question: What happens—

(a) if two players agree on a draw and announce their decision to the arbiter and then find, when the envelope is opened, that an illegal move has been recorded, or

(b) when one of the players in an adjourned game notifies the arbiter in writing that he resigns and then finds, when the envelope is opened, that his opponent has recorded an illegal move?

Answer: In case (a) the draw is still valid. In case (b) the resignation is still valid.

16.3. If the player having the move is absent, his clock shall be started, but the envelope shall be opened only at the time of his arrival.

16.4. If the player who has sealed the move is absent, the player having the move is not obliged to reply to the sealed move on the chessboard. He has the right to record his move in reply on his scoresheet, to put the scoresheet in an envelope, to stop his clock, and to start his opponent's clock. The envelope should then be put into safekeeping and opened on the opponent's arrival.

FIDE INTERPRETATION ART. 16.4 (1958). Question: What happens in the case when, in the situation described in Article 16.4, a player has sealed a move, the real significance of which it is impossible to establish?

Answer: The Commission declares that this case is governed by Article 17.3.

16.5. If the envelope containing the move recorded in accordance with Article 16.4 has disappeared, the game shall be resumed from the position at the time of adjournment and with the clock times recorded at the time of adjournment.

If the envelope containing the move sealed on adjournment has disappeared without it being possible to reestablish the position and the times used for the adjourned game, or if for any

other reason the said position and the said times cannot be reestablished, the game is annulled, and a new game must be played instead of the adjourned game.

FIDE INTERPRETATION ART. 16.5 (1970). Question: What measures should be taken when the conditions indicated in Article 16.5 are only partially fulfilled, in that the envelope containing the sealed move has disappeared, but it is still possible to establish by an agreement between the players the position at the adjournment and the times used until that moment?

Answer: The Commission decides that the game under such circumstances has to be continued.

16.6. If, upon resumption of the game, the time used has been incorrectly indicated on either clock, and if either player points this out before making his first move, the error must be corrected. If the error is not so established, the game continues without correction.

FIDE INTERPRETATION ART. 16.6 (1976). The Commission points out that checking the times on the clocks before play (at the beginning of the game as well as upon resumption) is a responsibility of the players. If they neglect to check the times indicated on the clocks, they must bear the consequences of their negligence, unless the arbiter feels that, in a particular case, these consequences would be too severe.

ARTICLE 17 · THE LOSS OF THE GAME

A game is lost by a player—
1. who has not played the prescribed number of moves in the given time,

FIDE INTERPRETATION ART. 17.1 (1970). With reference to the General Observations (FIDE Interpretation Art. 1

[1959]), the Commission expresses the opinion that special regulations should be allowed insofar as they are required for conducting tournaments in which the number of players is large and the number of arbiters is rather small, so that the procedure to determine whether a player has lost a game under Article 17.1 cannot be observed.

USCF TOURNAMENT RULES ART. 17.1 (1–6). TIME-FORFEITS: USCF PROCEDURE.

USCF TOURNAMENT RULE 17.1 (1). *Only the opponent may concern himself with the possibility that a player has lost a game on time. Spectators and especially players in other games are prohibited from speaking or otherwise interfering in possible time-forfeit situations.*

USCF TOURNAMENT RULE 17.1 (2). *If it is convenient, a director should be present at any game in which both players are in time-trouble, in order that he may witness the players and take immediate action if a claim of a win on time is made by one of the players.*

A director must never initiate a time-forfeit without a player's having first made a claim. *(Exception: If the condition specified for the use of the Variation [FIDE Procedure], that officials can be present at all games in which there is time-trouble, applies and if the director has made the required prior announcement that he will use the Variation, the director acts under the procedures of the Variation.)*

(The USCF Procedure must be used in its entirety in all USCF-rated tournaments, unless the requirements for using the Variation [FIDE Procedure] have been met, in which case that Variation must be used in its entirety. The rules do not permit a combination of the two, whereby, e.g., the director acts under the Variation in those games where he is present and under the USCF Procedure in those games where he is not present.)

USCF TOURNAMENT RULE 17.1 (3). *Under this rule the flag is considered to have fallen when a claim to that effect has been made by a player (see FIDE Interpretation 14.4 [1974]), not necessarily when the flag actually fell. The director's decision is made on the basis of the conditions existing at the time the claim of a win on time is made by a player.*

USCF TOURNAMENT RULE 17.1 (4). *When the flag of a player's clock falls at the expiration of his time-control period and his opponent claims that he has not completed the prescribed number of moves, play in the game ceases, but neither player is permitted to stop the clocks (see USCF Tournament Rule 14.6 [1]) without becoming subject to the director's discretionary power to penalize for infractions of the rules. (The director, if he is not present at the time, is empowered to adjust the clocks later if he feels it is justifiable, under the same rule.)*

The player may accept the claim of his opponent by signing a scoresheet bearing the result accepted or by otherwise acknowledging his loss in the manner specified by the director (see USCF Tournament Rule 13.1 [3]).

USCF TOURNAMENT RULE 17.1 (5). *If the player does not accept the claim—*

(a) If a director is present, he stops both clocks and rules on whether or not the player has lost the game under the provisions of USCF Tournament Rule Art. 17.1 (6). If the director rules not to forfeit the player, he starts the clock of the player having the move, and the game continues (or is adjourned) as specified in (6c).

(b) If a director is not present, the opponent must not fill in any previous moves missing from his scoresheet and must immediately summon a director to the board. When the director arrives, he proceeds in the manner specified in (a).

If both flags have fallen by the time the director arrives, a claim of a win on time may be considered only if the opponent's own clock is running and the director is satisfied that the opponent did not stop his own clock and start the player's clock after the player's flag was claimed to have fallen; otherwise, the claim is void and the game continues (or is adjourned) as specified in (6c).

If the flag of a player's clock falls at the expiration of his time-control period and his opponent's scoresheet is unsatisfactory to claim a win on time, the player himself may call the situation to the attention of a director (or an impartial witness pending the director's arrival), even in the absence of a claim by his opponent, in order to protect himself against a possible subsequent claim during the same time-control period.

USCF TOURNAMENT RULE 17.1 (6). *Under the conditions specified in USCF Tournament Rule 17.1 (5), a player loses the game by time-forfeit and his opponent is ruled the winner if the following provisions are satisfied.*

(a) *The opponent must have a complete score of the game. (The director may permit up to three incomplete move-pairs if written and also, wherever possible, oral announcement is made in advance of the first round of the number of move-lines that may be missing. A move-pair is defined as two consecutive moves, one for White and one for Black; three consecutive missing moves are counted as two move-pairs. If either side's move is omitted, a move-pair is counted as incomplete. Incomplete move-pairs may occur at any point in the game and are not limited to the last moves before the claim.)*

Until the opponent is requested by the director to fill in the incomplete move-pairs referred to in the preceding paragraph (moves so recorded may not be used to substantiate the opponent's claim), the opponent should not have filled in any previous moves missing from his scoresheet after the claim was made. Moves filled in in violation of this principle may not count toward the completeness of the opponent's scoresheet, and if it is established that the opponent filled in moves after the claim was made, but their number cannot be proved, the player must be given the benefit of the doubt concerning the number of moves thus improperly recorded by the opponent, but not beyond the highest figure in the doubtful range. The last move-pair before the claim is not considered a previous move missing which cannot be filled in, but may properly be recorded without voiding the claim.

Any moves written down before a claim by either player that a flag has fallen are not regarded as the filling in of previous moves missing, but as properly recorded moves. Therefore, the claim is not voided by recording such moves.

(b) The opponent must have a scoresheet which is playable (reasonably legible and accurate) in the opinion of the director under his discretionary powers. Individual unplayable moves recorded are counted against the completeness of the move-pair involved.

Examples of errors which do not affect the playability of the score are minor technical errors (e.g., ambiguous moves), errors involving one wrong symbol (unless the actual move is disputed or the error is repeated to the extent that the whole score becomes ambiguous).

Examples of errors which do affect the playability of the score: errors involving more than one wrong symbol (unless the piece named is correct and the only move possible is given incorrectly), white moves in the black column and vice versa (only the original error is counted). Check marks, which have no legal standing whatsoever, and blank spaces are never acceptable, even when the player has only one legal move.

(c) The opponent's scoresheet, after verification if necessary, must prove that the player whose flag fell had not completed the given number of moves. The player may volunteer his own scoresheet to disprove the opponent's claim.

If all the provisions stated in this rule are not fulfilled, no time-forfeit shall be ruled, and the game shall continue (or be adjourned) from the final position as if the next time-control period had commenced (see USCF Tournament Rule Art. 15.1 [1a]) and from the first move number of the next time-control period, unless the director can establish exactly the number of moves made. With the commencement of each new time-control period, each player is afforded anew the opportunity to claim a win on time against his opponent, whether or not the scoresheet has been completed from previous time-controls (see USCF Tournament Rule Art. 13.2 [1]), and no further claims of a win on time from the previous time-control period are permitted.

USCF TOURNAMENT RULE ART. 17.1 (2)—VARIATION (FIDE PROCEDURE). *In a tournament in which directors can be present at all games where there is time-trouble, the follow-*

ing procedure may be substituted. However, written and also, whenever possible, oral announcement must be made in advance of the first round.

A director will count the final moves of the game as they are played. When a player's flag falls, that player will be forfeited if the director's count shows that the player has not made the prescribed number of moves. An appeal from the director's decision must be accompanied by a complete score of the game.

2. who arrives at the chessboard more than one hour late,

FIDE INTERPRETATION ART. 17.2 (1958). In the case where a player or team of players arrives late for a competition, the Commission deems that it should stand by the principles of the General Observations (FIDE Interpretation Art. 1 [1959]). If the delay is due to a cause for which the players are not responsible, then it must follow from the principle of sportsmanship in chess, at least in international tournaments, that concessions should be granted as far as it is possible to do so without creating eventual difficulties to other players or to the organizers.

FIDE INTERPRETATION ART. 17.2 (1962). The Commission declares that the stipulations of Article 17.2 and 17.4 of the Laws of Chess, stating that a game is lost for players arriving at the chessboard more than one hour late, are applicable as much at the commencement of a game as on resumption of play after an adjournment. In the opinion of the Commission, there cannot be any difficulty in applying this rule in the situation in which, on resumption of an adjourned game, the player who has sealed a move is absent while his opponent presents himself at the chessboard. If the former is still absent after the lapse of one hour, the game is lost for him unless it has been decided previously by one of three circumstances, viz.—

(a) the absent player has won the game by virtue of the fact that the sealed move is checkmate,

(b) the absent player has produced a drawn game by virtue of the fact that the sealed move is stalemate, or

(c) the player present at the chessboard has lost the game according to Article 17.1 by exceeding his time-limit.

Basically, this declaration by the Commission implies a mere substantiation of the evident fact that what happens in consequence of an action or of an omission after the termination of a game is without importance.

FIDE INTERPRETATION ART. 17.2 (1966). Question: If in adjourning a game, a player has some remaining time in his favor (more than one hour), should his opponent, when the game is continued, wait an hour or wait until the full time which the player has in his favor has elapsed before claiming a win in case of the player's nonappearance?

Answer: This case has already been solved by FIDE Interpretation Art. 17.2 (1962).

USCF TOURNAMENT RULE ART. 17.2 (1). *Any player who does not notify a director in advance that he will be unable to play in any round and then defaults the game by not appearing within one hour after the starting time (FIDE Article 17.2) may be fined the sum of $5.00, payable to the sponsoring organization. The player should not be permitted to continue play in the tournament and may be barred by the sponsoring organization from any of its tournaments until the fine is paid.*

3. who has sealed a move the real significance of which it is impossible to establish, or

FIDE INTERPRETATION ART. 17.3 (1958). Having been asked for a more precise formulation of Article 17.3, the Commission once again refers to the General Observations (FIDE Interpretation Art. 1 [1959]). It is the duty of the arbiter to make the necessary decision in accordance with the circumstances of each particular case.

FIDE INTERPRETATION ART. 17.3 (1965). According to the opinion of the Commission, it ought to be clearly established by the wording of this Article that not only when the notation is inexact but also when a clear notation indicates an irregular move, it is incumbent on the arbiter to judge whether there exists any reasonable doubt as to the move which the player has intended to indicate.

FIDE INTERPRETATION ART. 17.3 (1975). Question: In a recent tournament Player A was asked to seal a move of adjournment. Player A subsequently handed his sealed-move envelope to the arbiter, who kept it in his custody. When the adjourned game was resumed, the envelope was opened, but only the scoresheet of Player B was found in the envelope. The arbiter ruled that Player A's failure to seal his move automatically entailed the loss of the game under Article 17.3. Was the arbiter's ruling correct?

Answer: Yes. It should be remarked, however, that the arbiter (or one of his assistants) should be blamed, as he did not make sure that the scoresheet of Player A was in the envelope, even though it was his duty to do so.

FIDE INTERPRETATION ART. 17.3 (1976). Question: According to FIDE Interpretation Art. 17.3 (1958), the arbiter has the duty of deciding the real significance of a sealed move. This is undesirable, as the arbiter should interfere as little as possible in the game and should serve only to see that neither player gains an unfair advantage from his mistakes. What is the opinion of the Commission?

Answer: The player sealing a move should be aware that the responsibility for sealing a correct move is entirely *his* and that if he seals an illegal or ambiguous move, he may lose the game.

4. who during the game refuses to comply with the Laws.

If both players refuse to comply with the Laws or if both players arrive at the chessboard more than one hour late, the game shall be declared lost by both players.

ARTICLE 18 · THE DRAWN GAME

18.1. A proposal of a draw under the provisions of Article 12.2 may be made by a player only at the moment when he has just

completed a move. On then proposing a draw, he starts the
clock of his opponent. The latter may accept the proposal or,
either orally or by completing a move, he may reject it; in the
interval the player who has made the proposal cannot withdraw it.

FIDE INTERPRETATION ART. 18.1 (1974A). A proposal to
draw not made in accordance with Article 18.1 is treated as
follows—

(a) if a player proposes a draw while his opponent's clock
is running, the opponent may agree to the draw or reject the
offer; or

(b) if a player proposes a draw while his own clock is running, the opponent may accept or reject the offer, or he may
postpone his decision until after the player has completed a
move.

In these situations the opponent may reject the proposal orally
or by completing a move at his first opportunity. In the interval
between the offer of a draw and the opponent's acceptance of it,
the player who made the proposal cannot withdraw it.

FIDE INTERPRETATION ART. 18.1 (1974B). A player proposed a draw and made his move on the board before his opponent had replied to the offer. The opponent, after some minutes'
consideration, accepted the offer. The arbiter rendered the
player's proposal valid and thus proclaimed the game drawn.
One of the arguments for this decision was that the proposal
maintained its validity since the proposal itself is more important
than the form.

The Commission disagrees with the last-mentioned argument,
since here the way the draw is offered is the thing that matters.
In spite of the reasoning offered, the Commission approves the
actual decision taken in this particular case.

The Commission thinks that this matter has adequately been
covered by FIDE Interpretation Art. 18.1 (1974A).

FIDE INTERPRETATIONS ART. 18.1 (1959, 1960, 1963,
1964). THE QUESTION OF PREMATURE DRAWS.

FIDE INTERPRETATION ART. 18.1 (1959). From a sporting point of view, it is quite inappropriate that a game be finished before a real fight has commenced; competition ought to imply that every player should try to fight in order to win his game until the moment when the situation does not afford any further hope of victory.

Attention is drawn in particular to the fact that in this respect the International Grandmasters and the International Masters of FIDE ought to serve as examples to the other players. Players who repeatedly act without respecting their duty to the organizers and to the chess public may be subject to disciplinary measures taken by the arbiter.

FIDE INTERPRETATION ART. 18.1 (1960). It is hardly possible to establish prescriptions sufficiently detailed to be directly applicable to each particular case. On the basis of the general principle that the players may not ignore the necessity of an honest fight, the examination of each particular case ought, according to the opinion of the Commission, to devolve upon the person who is in charge of the tournament in which the game in question has been played. At this examination it must not be forgotten that a player may have quite legitimate reasons—his actual situation in the tournament table, his state of health, etc.—for desisting from whatever prospects he has in a given situation for continuing the game to a victory and that he may therefore be considered entitled to make or accept an offer of a draw.

FIDE INTERPRETATION ART. 18.1 (1963). It seems necessary to stipulate clearly and in writing certain moral principles which should guide the game, but are not incorporated in the Laws, in order to enable the arbiter to secure as far as possible a fair, sportsmanlike contest.

The Commission emphasizes the following points.

(a) Every agreement to draw should, as a matter of principle, be based on a position on the chessboard which, in the opinion of each of the two players, offers no tangible possibility of pursuing the game to a victorious conclusion without running an obvious risk of defeat.

(b) Particular circumstances may exist, however, which should authorize a player to propose or accept a draw in cases differing from those mentioned in (a). It is not possible to define these particular circumstances in a complete manner, just as in the official regulations the stipulations governing agreements to draw should, in the opinion of the Commission, be so conceived as to comprise only basic principles and goals, as competent arbiters must be presumed to know how to apply them to concrete cases in an equitable manner.

The principles so formulated relate to a basic principle, according to which each player should conduct his whole game as a fight for the best possible result. Voluntary measures to evade the fight or to favor the opponent or a third player should be held contemptible for reasons of sport and be judged accordingly.

It is easy to establish that it is difficult, in certain cases even impossible, to judge correctly the measures to be taken in situations varying in character, and the arbiter should impose penalties only in cases which clearly constitute contraventions of the moral principles involved.

FIDE INTERPRETATION ART. 18.1 (1964). An agreement to draw a game before the 30th move in many cases involves an act which rightly could be deemed contradictory to the stated principles on premature draws. Arbiters are requested to impose, in cases where clear contraventions of the moral principles of the game are demonstrated, penalties as severe as loss of the game.

USCF TOURNAMENT RULE ART. 18.1 (1). *A player who does not conform to the specifications of Article 18.1 when proposing a draw by agreement (Article 12.2) is breaking the Laws of Chess and should be penalized or warned at the discretion of the director.*

USCF TOURNAMENT RULE ART. 18.1 (2). *It is unethical and unsportsmanlike to agree to a draw before a serious contest has begun. The same is true of all agreements to prearrange game results. In cases of clear violations of the moral principles of the game, a director should impose penalties at his discretion.*

18.2. If a player claims a draw under the provisions of Article 12.3, his clock must continue to run until the arbiter has verified the legitimacy of the claim.

If the claim is found to be correct, the game shall be declared drawn, even if the claimant, in the interval, has overstepped the time-limit.

If the claim is found to be incorrect, the game shall continue, unless the claimant has, in the interval, overstepped the time-limit, in which case the game will be declared lost by the claimant.

FIDE INTERPRETATION ART. 18.2 (1974). Question: What happens when an arbiter—

(a) accepts a claim of a draw, but then is proved to have made a mistake; or

(b) turns down a claim of a draw which afterwards proves to have been correct?

Answer: If a claim of a draw has been mistakenly accepted by the arbiter and a higher authority subsequently rejects the claim, then the player who has not claimed the draw is entitled to resume the game.

If a claim of a draw has been refused by the arbiter, then the player who has made the claim is entitled to stop playing and appeal to a higher authority. If then the player's claim is proved to be incorrect, the game shall be declared lost for that player.

FIDE INTERPRETATION ART. 18.2 (1976). Question: A player who claims a draw by repetition under Article 12.3 and asks the arbiter to verify the legitimacy of the claim while the clock continues to run in accordance with Article 18.2 is dependent upon the chess-playing ability of the arbiter as to the time taken for the verification. The outcome of the game may thus be determined by the arbiter's ability, yet no arbiter is required to have such ability. What is the opinion of the Commission?

Answer: The Commission agrees that in order to make consistent for all players the time taken to verify the legitimacy of a claim of a draw by repetition of position under Article 12.3, but at the same time to discourage frivolous claims of such a type, the claimant is charged exactly five minutes on his clock for the verification. If the claim is found to be incorrect, the provisions of Article 18.2 for this case apply after the five minutes have been charged.

ARTICLE 19 · THE CONDUCT OF THE PLAYERS

19.1. (a) During play the players are forbidden to make use of handwritten or printed matter or to analyze the game on another chessboard; they are also forbidden to have resource to the advice or opinion of a third party, whether solicited or not.

FIDE INTERPRETATION ART. 19.1a (1960). The Commission shares the opinion that the result of a game of chess ought to depend exclusively on the actual strength of each player and that consequently the collaboration of others ought to be allowed no more after an adjournment than in the course of the game at the chessboard. It must, however, be observed that whereas in the playing rooms perfect control can be upheld, this is not possible during the time the game is adjourned. It must therefore be held in mind that a general prohibition of the use of seconds would probably not be respected by all players and that in practice it might be disadvantageous for those players who would loyally respect the prohibition.

Thus, the only effective and just means of eliminating, as far as possible, the use of seconds probably consists in a change of the system for the organization of tournaments.

FIDE INTERPRETATION ART. 19.1a (1975). Question: In a time-trouble game the captain of one side informed (without being asked to do so) the player of his side (White) that his opponent had just completed the last move of the prescribed series of moves. As a consequence of this, White had now enough time to think his position over. He found the winning continuation in the rather complicated position.

Black felt that his chances had been damaged by the action of the captain of the opposite side, particularly as in the time-trouble phase of the game the chances for a win changed continuously. In this phase of the game, both players did not write down their moves and did not even mark the number of moves they played.

The appeals committee did not accept the protest of Black and gave the motives for its decision by referring to many international tournaments where the players, the arbiter, and other persons present in the tournament hall can see continuously the position and the number of moves made on the big wall boards. The committee said that everyone had the right to inform the players at any time about the number of moves completed, as long as there is no infringement of Article 19.1a of the Laws.

Here follow three specific questions:

(a) When may a player be informed about the number of moves he has made (before or after the time-control)?

(b) Who has the right (or is obliged) to give that information (the arbiter, the team captain, other persons)?

(c) What kind of penalty should be given in connection with the abovementioned parties for incorrect behavior?

Answer:

(a) Never.

(b) Nobody.

(c) This is left to the discretion of the arbiter.

(But see FIDE Interpretation Art. 13.2 [1976] for the procedure at time-control.)

FIDE INTERPRETATION ART. 19.1a (1976A). The prohibition against handwritten or printed matter applies not only to what is brought in from the outside but also to notes made during play which could in any way serve as an aid to memory. Aside from the actual recording of the moves, only the addition of an objective fact such as the time on the clocks is permitted.

FIDE INTERPRETATION ART. 19.1a (1976B). Question:

How is Article 19.1a to be applied in the case of a team competition and more specifically, what actions are permissible for a team captain while play is in progress?

Answer: The role of the team captain is basically an administrative one. According to the regulations of the competition, the captain may be required to do such things as deliver to an arbiter a written list giving the players of his team who will participate in each round, see that those of his players who are not taking part in the current match or those who have finished their games are not present in the space reserved for the players, report the results of a match to an arbiter at the end of play, etc.

In principle, the captain must abstain from any intervention during play. He should not, by virtue of his own playing strength, give information to a player concerning the position on the chessboard of that or any other player, since the captain would then be giving information to a member of his team on the play of the game which the team member's own abilities might not have allowed him to discover for himself.

The captain is, by the weight of practice, entitled to advise the players of his team to make or to accept an offer of a draw or to resign a game, on condition that he does not make any comments concerning the actual position on the chessboard. He must confine himself to giving only brief information which can in no way be interpreted by the player as an opinion on the game, but might instead be interpreted as based on any number of circumstances pertaining to the match.

In addition to the captain's being prohibited from expressing an opinion on the state of the game to any other person, he is also prohibited from consulting any other person as to the state of the game, just as players are subject to the same prohibitions.

The captain may say to a player, "Offer a draw," "Accept the draw," or "Resign the game," but this brief information should be given in a general way and not in any way that may be interpreted as an opinion on the state of the game. For example, if asked by a player whether he should accept an offer of a draw, the captain should not begin to analyze for himself any board in such a way that his reply could be interpreted as an opinion on the position.

Even though in a team competition there is a certain team loyalty which goes beyond a player's individual game, a game of chess is, at base, a competition between two players. Therefore, the player must have the final say over the play of his own game. Although the advice of the captain should weigh heavily with the player, the player is not absolutely compelled to abide by that advice. Likewise, the captain cannot act on behalf of a player and his game without the knowledge and consent of the player.

(b) No analysis is permitted in the playing rooms during play or during adjourned sessions.

(c) It is forbidden to distract or annoy the opponent in any manner whatsoever.

FIDE INTERPRETATION ART. 19.1c (1958). Article 19.1c should be applied in the case where a player who has proposed a draw reiterates his proposal without reasons that are clearly well-founded before the opponent has, in his turn, made use of his right to propose a draw.

Article 19.1c protects the players sufficiently, and the application of this Article can always be requested from the arbiter against a player who proposes a draw too frequently to his opponent.

USCF TOURNAMENT RULE ART. 19.1c (1). *During playing sessions players with games in progress should not leave the playing room for extended periods without first informing the director.*

A player who does not wish to continue a lost game and leaves without being courteous enough to resign or to notify the director may be severely penalized, at the discretion of a director, for poor sportsmanship.

19.2. Infractions of the rules indicated in Article 19.1 may incur penalties even to the extent of loss of the game.

ARTICLE 20 · THE ARBITER OF THE COMPETITION

An arbiter should be designated to control the competition. His duties are—

1. to see that the Laws are strictly observed;

USCF TOURNAMENT RULE ART. 20.1 (1). *The competition must be supervised by a chief tournament director, who must be a USCF Certified Tournament Director at the level required by the type of tournament. The chief director, on behalf of the sponsoring affiliate, is responsible for the technical management of the tournament and is bound by the Laws, by the FIDE Interpretations of the Laws, by the USCF Tournament Rules and Pairing Rules, and by all USCF procedures and policies.*

The chief director's duties and powers normally include the following: to appoint assistants of various types as required to perform his duties, to accept and list entries, to establish suitable conditions of play and to announce them to the participants, to collect scores and tabulate results, and to report results to the sponsoring organization and the USCF for the official record.

The chief director may delegate any of his duties to assistants, but he is not thereby relieved of responsibility for their correct performance. A tournament director, as he must have absolute objectivity and must be able to devote his full attention to his duties as director, should not, on principle, be a player in any tournament he directs. At the lowest level of tournaments, the director may be a player in the tournament if necessary, but a director who is not a player in the tournament is recommended whenever possible. The chief director is strictly prohibited from being a player in any tournament above the lowest level.

USCF TOURNAMENT RULE ART. 20.1 (2). *The following exception to normal procedure applies only to large tournaments in which it is impossible to supervise play in all games: In general, it is not always possible to enforce Interpretations or Tournament Rules that depend on constant supervision of a game, but if a director witnesses a violation of any Law, Interpretation, or Tournament Rule, it is his duty to require compliance and, at his discretion, to penalize the guilty player.*

2. to supervise the progress of the competition, to establish that the prescribed time-limit has not been exceeded by the players, to arrange the order of resumption of play in adjourned games, to see that the arrangements contained in Article 15 are observed (above all to see that the information on the envelope is correct), to keep the sealed-move envelope until the time when the adjourned game is resumed, etc.;

3. to enforce the decisions he may make in disputes that have arisen during the course of the competition; and

FIDE INTERPRETATION ART. 20.3 (1958). The Commission considers that there is no need to include in the Laws prescriptions concerning appeals against the decision of an arbiter. However, when it is a question of international tournaments, it is doubtless appropriate to have a committee at the place where the competition takes place entrusted with the task of resolving disputes in the event of appeals against an arbiter's decision.

USCF TOURNAMENT RULES ART. 20.3 (1–4). APPEALS.

USCF TOURNAMENT RULE ART. 20.3 (1). *A player may appeal any ruling made by the chief director or one of his assistants, provided that the appeal is promptly made after the ruling before the appellant completes another move. All appeals must be made in writing through the chief director. Any appeal not meeting these requirements is void.*

If the chief director reserves his decision temporarily and directs that play continue before the appeal is heard, the appellant must continue play "under protest," i.e., without prejudice to his appeal regardless of the outcome of further play. However, every effort should be made to resolve an appeal before the director requires that play proceed.

USCF TOURNAMENT RULE ART. 20.3 (2). *If the chief director believes that the appeal is justified, he may reverse or modify any previous decision made by himself or one of his assistants.*

If he does not believe that the appeal is justified and so advises the appellant, who nevertheless wishes to pursue the appeal further—

(a) When an appeals committee cannot meet without disturbing the orderly progress of the tournament or when the appeal deals solely with a point of law, the chief director hears and rules upon the appeal. A player whose appeal on a point of law has been ruled upon adversely by the director may appeal through the USCF National Office as specified in (4).

(b) In any other case, the director must appoint a committee of three persons (preferably including at least one USCF Certified Tournament Director) to which to refer the appeal, as specified in (3). The committee must consist of disinterested persons and be selected in consultation with the appellant and his opponent. If the committee finds that the appeal is clearly groundless, it may authorize the director to penalize the player for that reason. The committee may either specify the penalty or leave it to the director's final determination.

USCF Tournament Rule Art. 20.3 (3). *When an appeals committee hears an appeal, all persons except the members of the committee, the chief director, the appellant, his opponent, and the testifying witnesses should be excluded from the hearing. When the committee hears an appeal, it must give pre-eminent weight to the director's testimony as to anything said or done in his presence.*

The committee hears and rules upon such part of an appeal as involves questions of fact or the exercise of the director's discretionary powers. The appeals committee's decision should be transmitted in writing to the director and signed by the committee members.

In ruling on an appeal, the committee may exercise all powers, but only those powers, accorded to the director, except that the committee may not overrule the director's ruling on a point of law. However, if the committee determines that a decision on a point of law must be immediately appealed during the tournament to avoid serious, irreparable consequences (or when large cash prizes are at stake), it may, by a unanimous vote, appeal the director's ruling on a point of law through the USCF National Office, which will follow established procedures for dealing with the appeal.

USCF TOURNAMENT RULE ART. 20.3 (4). *Only if the prescribed procedures have been properly exhausted may a further appeal be made through the USCF National Office on a point of law (there is no appeal through the National Office permitted on a question of fact or the director's exercise of his discretionary powers, which is heard and ruled upon only at the tournament). The appellant must make the appeal in writing and mail it within seven days of the ruling to the National Office, which will follow established procedures for dealing with the appeal.*

4. to impose penalties on the players for any fault or infraction of the Laws.

USCF TOURNAMENT RULE ART. 20.4 (1). *A player has the right to call the director to rule upon a point of law, procedure, or conduct. In all cases in which the director is called, he should first attempt to establish the facts (in such a way that other games in progress are not disturbed).*

If the facts are agreed upon, the director should rule as follows:

(a) If no penalty is prescribed by law and there is no occasion for him to exercise his discretionary power to penalize, he should direct the players to proceed with play.

(b) If a case is clearly covered by a Law that specifies a penalty, he should enforce that penalty.

(c) If an infraction has occurred for which no penalty is prescribed by law, the director may exercise his discretionary power to penalize.

If the facts are not agreed upon, the director should proceed as follows:

(a) If the director is satisfied that he has ascertained the facts, he should rule accordingly.

(b) If the director is unable to determine the facts to his satisfaction, he must make a ruling that will permit play to continue and notify the players of their right to appeal.

Unbiased evidence is required to support any claim by a player that his opponent violated a Law. (See FIDE Interpretation Art. 8.2 [1972].)

If the director believes that an appeal of his ruling on a point of fact or the exercise of his discretionary power to penalize might be in order, he should advise a player of his right to appeal.

USCF TOURNAMENT RULE ART. 20.4 (2). *In case of a dispute, the director should make every effort to reach a resolution of the matter by informal, conciliatory means before he resorts to the exercise of his formal discretionary power to penalize. If such means fail, where penalties are not specifically defined by the Laws or the Tournament Rules, the director has discretionary power to impose penalties as follows for infractions and maintenance of discipline*

(a) issue a formal warning,

(b) fine a player any amount not to exceed $10.00, payable to the sponsoring organization (the player should not be permitted to continue play in the tournament and may be barred by the sponsoring organization from any of its tournaments until the fine is paid),

(c) advance the time on a player's clock or give his opponent additional time,

(d) cancel a game and rule that a new game be played in its stead,

(e) declare a game lost by a player and won by his opponent,

(f) declare a game lost by both players, or

(g) expel a player from the tournament.

ARTICLE 21 · THE INTERPRETATION OF THE LAWS

In case of doubt as to the application or interpretation of the Laws, FIDE will examine the evidence and render official decisions. Rulings published are binding on all affiliated federations.

FIDE INTERPRETATION ART. 21 (1957). INDIVIDUAL PRIZES IN TEAM TOURNAMENTS. When, in a team chess competition, special prizes are instituted for the best percentage results arrived at by individual players, only the results of participants who have played a number of rounds at least two-thirds of the total number of rounds are to be counted.

FIDE INTERPRETATION ART. 21 (1967). APPLICATION OF THE SONNENBORN-BERGER SYSTEM IN THE CASE OF A TIE IN A TEAM TOURNAMENT. Question: How is the Sonnenborn-Berger System to be applied in the case of a tie in a team tournament?

Answer: In the application of the Sonnenborn-Berger (Tie-Breaking) System to an individual tournament, every player is assigned a number of points calculated by a special rule. Specifically, each player is given the total number of points scored by each opponent he defeated and half the total number of points scored by each opponent with whom he drew. Three alternatives, then, are possible: a win giving the total number of points scored in the tournament by the opponent, a draw giving half that number of points, and a loss giving no points.

In a team tournament, when game points are being used, the number of alternatives possible depends upon the number of players on each team. For example, in a tournament where the number of players on each team is four, there are nine possible alternatives: 4, 3½, 3, 2½, 2, 1½, 1, ½, 0. If, in a tournament of this kind, two participating teams, A and B, have the same number of game points, whereas a third team, C, has 16 points, the Sonnenborn-Berger totals which Team A and Team B each obtained in their match with Team C are calculated as follows:

If the team scored	4	points	(100	%),	its S-B total is 16.
" " " "	3½	"	(87½	%),	" " " " 14.
" " " "	3	"	(75	%),	" " " " 12.
" " " "	2½	"	(62½	%),	" " " " 10.
" " " "	2	"	(50	%),	" " " " 8.
" " " "	1½	"	(37½	%),	" " " " 6.
" " " "	1	"	(25	%),	" " " " 4.
" " " "	½	"	(12½	%),	" " " " 2.
" " " "	0	"	(0	%),	" " " " 0.

FIDE INTERPRETATIONS ART. 21 (1970, 1973). CONSEQUENCES WHEN A PLAYER OR A TEAM WITHDRAWS OR IS EXPELLED FROM A TOURNAMENT.

FIDE INTERPRETATION ART. 21 (1970). Question: What are the consequences when a player or team withdraws or is expelled from a (round-robin) tournament?

Answer: If a player has not completed at least 50% of his games when he leaves the tournament, his score remains in the tournament table (for rating and historical purposes), but the points scored by him or against him are not counted in the final standings. For the games not played or finished, the player, as well as his opponent, get a /—/ in the tournament table.

If a player has completed at least 50% of his games when he leaves the tournament, his score remains in the tournament table and will be counted in the final standings. For the games not played the opponents will get a /1/ and the player himself will get a /0/.

The same rules apply equally when a team is concerned instead of a player.

FIDE INTERPRETATION ART. 21 (1973). Relating to a player's retirement from a tournament, chroniclers of events are at liberty to indicate in the tournament table whether the defeats of such a player were "actual" or "declared" (defaulted).

FIDE INTERPRETATION ART. 21 (1971). AWARDING OF PRIZES IN CASE OF WITHDRAWAL. The question of whether or not a player who withdraws from a match is still entitled to receive the loser's prize was not decided.

FIDE INTERPRETATIONS ART. 21 (1957, 1975). STANDARDS OF CHESS EQUIPMENT FOR FIDE TOURNAMENTS.

FIDE INTERPRETATION ART. 21 (1957). In a competition of FIDE, or one under FIDE auspices, it is recommended that the pieces be of the Staunton pattern or a similar pattern in order that the participants may recognize the pieces without confusion.

If the pieces would be different from those prescribed in the preceding paragraph and if one of the players or the captain of a team demands that the prescribed pattern be used, the utilization of that pattern is obligatory.

FIDE INTERPRETATION ART. 21 (1975). These regulations define the general standards for chess equipment to be used in FIDE competitions and apply only to the equipment used in FIDE competitions. Manufacturers of equipment and organizers are completely free to make and use equipment for all other competitions. Manufacturing is encouraged of all sets of artistic value, regardless of the practical possibilities of their use.

(a) Used in matches of two players shall be the chess pieces agreed upon by both. Their agreement shall also be observed concerning other equipment—chess table, board, and clock. In case the players disagree, the equipment to be used shall be decided by the chief arbiter of the match, who shall bear in mind the following standards for size and form.

(b) Used in the tournaments, Olympiads, and other competitions within the FIDE system shall be the chess equipment offered by the organizers (hosts) of a particular competition, provided that it conforms to the following standards and has been approved by the chief arbiter.

Chess Pieces.

Material. Chess pieces should be made of wood, plastic, or an imitation of these materials.

Height, Weight, Proportions. The king's height should be 8.5 to 10.5 cm. The diameter of the king's base should measure 40 to 50% of the height. The size of the other pieces should be proportionate to their height and form. Other elements, such as stability, aesthetic considerations, etc., may also be taken into account. The weight of the pieces should be suitable for comfortable moving and stability.

Form, Style of Make. Recommended for use in FIDE competitions are those types of chess sets and equipment which have already been used in Men's Olympiads, Interzonal Tournaments, Candidates' Matches and Tournaments, and World Championship Matches. The pieces should be shaped so as to be clearly distinguishable from one another. In particular, the top of the king should differ distinctly from that of the queen. The top of the bishop may bear a notch or be of a special color clearly distinguishing it from a pawn.

Color of Chess Pieces. The dark pieces should be brown or black in color or dark shades of these colors. The light pieces may be white or cream or other light colors. The natural color of wood (walnut, maple, etc.) may also be used for this purpose. The pieces should not be shiny and should be pleasing to the eye.

Chessboards.

Material. Wood, plastic, cardboard, or cloth are recommended as material for chessboards. The board may also be of stone (marble) with appropriate light and dark colors, provided that the chief arbiter has found it acceptable. Natural wood with sufficient contrast, such as birch, maple, or European ash against walnut, teak, beech, etc., may also be used for boards, which must have a dull or neutral finish, never shiny.

Color of Chessboards. Combinations of colors, such as brown, green, or very light tan and white, cream, off-white ivory, buff, etc., may be used for the squares in addition to natural colors.

Proportions. The board size should be such that the pieces appear neither too crowded nor too lonely on the squares. It is recommended that the side of a square measure 5.0 to 6.5 cm.

Tables. A table, comfortable and of suitable height, may be fitted with a chessboard. If the table and board are separate from one another, the latter must be fastened and thus prevented from moving during play.

Chess Clocks.

Chess clocks should have a device signaling precisely when the hour hand indicates full hours. They should have the flag fixed at the figure 12 or at some other figure, but always so that its fall can be clearly seen, helping the arbiters and players to check the time. The clock should have no shine making the flag poorly visible. It should work as silently as possible, in order not to disturb the players during play.

FIDE INTERPRETATION ART. 21 (1976). TIE-BREAKING. The Commission recommends that tie-breaking be avoided if possible. For the purposes of published crosstables, tied players should be indicated as such and arranged in a convenient way, e.g., alphabetically. In those cases when tie-breaking must be used, such as to award a single trophy, the organizers should announce in advance which methods will be used for breaking the ties, and these methods should be included in the regulations for the tournament.

USCF TOURNAMENT RULE ART. 21 (1). *The standards of chess equipment for FIDE tournaments are applicable also to USCF tournaments. Unless the organizers have provided standard equipment or designated preferred equipment for all players, Black has his choice of any equipment conforming to these standards. If Black is absent when the round begins and White arrives first, White has the choice. The opponent may not challenge the choice as not conforming unless he can provide or obtain equipment which does conform, or conforms more nearly to these standards. If the opponent has arrived late, his clock should continue running during any such challenge. Questionable cases are left to the discretion of the director.*

Supplements to the Laws

SUPPLEMENT NO. 1
THE NOTATION OF CHESS GAMES

FIDE recognizes for its own tournaments and matches only one system of notation, the algebraic system, and recommends the use of this uniform chess notation also for chess literature and periodicals. Scoresheets using a notation system other than the algebraic may not be used as evidence in cases where normally the scoresheet of a player is used for that purpose. An arbiter who observes that a player is using any other notation system than the algebraic should warn the player in question of this requirement.*

Description of the Algebraic System

1. Each piece is indicated by the first letter, a capital letter, of its name. Example: K = king, Q = queen, R = rook, B = bishop, N = knight.†

2. For the first letter of the name of a piece, each player is free to use the first letter of the name which is commonly used in his country. Examples: F = fou (French for bishop), L = loper (Dutch for bishop). In printed publications, the use of figurines for the pieces is recommended.

♚ ♛ ♜ ♝ ♞

---

* The provisions of this paragraph become effective on January 1, 1981. Until that date the descriptive system and the long form of the algebraic system are recognized, mainly to give those federations in which the descriptive notation is customary ample opportunity to introduce the algebraic notation within the realms of their federations. Each federation should do its utmost to promote the algebraic notation, the simple rules of which are given in this Supplement. Furthermore, each federation should do its utmost to urge the organizers of tournaments and matches other than those of FIDE within its realm to follow the provisions of this Supplement.

† In the case of the knight, for convenience sake, N is used.

3. Pawns are not indicated by their first letter, but are recognized by the absence of such a letter. Examples: e5, d4, a5.
4. The eight files (from left to right for White and from right to left for Black) are indicated by the small letters *a, b, c, d, e, f, g,* and *h,* respectively.
5. The eight ranks (from bottom to top for White and from top to bottom for Black) are numbered *1, 2, 3, 4, 5, 6, 7,* and *8,* respectively. Consequently, in the initial position the white pieces and pawns are placed on the first and second ranks; the black pieces and pawns on the eighth and seventh ranks.
6. As a consequence of the previous rules, each of the sixty-four squares is invariably indicated by a unique combination of a letter and a number.

Black

	a	b	c	d	e	f	g	h
8	a8	b8	c8	d8	e8	f8	g8	h8
7	a7	b7	c7	d7	e7	f7	g7	h7
6	a6	b6	c6	d6	e6	f6	g6	h6
5	a5	b5	c5	d5	e5	f5	g5	h5
4	a4	b4	c4	d4	e4	f4	g4	h4
3	a3	b3	c3	d3	e3	f3	g3	h3
2	a2	b2	c2	d2	e2	f2	g2	h2
1	a1	b1	c1	d1	e1	f1	g1	h1

White

7. Each move of a piece is indicated by (a) the first letter of the piece in question and (b) the square of arrival. There is no hyphen between (a) and (b). Examples: Be5, Nf3, Rd1.

In the case of pawns, only the square of arrival is indicated. Examples: e5, d4, a5.

8. When a piece makes a capture, an *x* is inserted between (a) the first letter of the piece in question and (b) the square of arrival. Examples: Bxe5, Nxf3, Rxd1.

When a pawn makes a capture, not only the square of arrival but also the file of departure must be indicated, followed by an *x*. Examples: dxe5, gxf3, axb5. In the case of an "en passant" capture, the square of arrival is given as the square on which the capturing pawn finally rests and "e.p." is appended to the notation.

9. If two identical pieces can move to the same square, the piece that is moved is indicated as follows:

(1) If both pieces are on the same rank: by (a) the first letter of the name of the piece, (b) the file of departure, and (c) the square of arrival.

(2) If both pieces are on the same file: by (a) the first letter of the name of the piece, (b) the number of the square of departure, and (c) the square of arrival.

(3) If the pieces are on different ranks and files, method (1) is preferred.

In case of a capture, an *x* must be inserted between (b) and (c).

Examples:

(1) There are two knights, on the squares g1 and d2, and one of them moves to the square f3: either Ngf3 or Ndf3, as the case may be.

(2) There are two knights, on the squares g5 and g1, and one of them moves to the square f3: either N5f3 or N1f3, as the case may be.

(3) There are two knights, on the squares h2 and d4, and one of them moves to the square f3: either Nhf3 or Ndf3, as the case may be.

If a capture takes place on the square f3, the previous examples are changed by the insertion of an *x:* (1) either Ngxf3 or Ndxf3, (2) either N5xf3 or N1xf3, (3) either Nhxf3 or Ndxf3, as the case may be.

10. If two pawns can capture the same piece or pawn of the opponent, the pawn that is moved is indicated by (1) the letter of the file of departure, (b) an *x,* and (c) the square of arrival. Example: If there are white pawns on the squares c4 and e4 and a black pawn or piece on the square d5, the notation for White's move is either cxd5 or exd5, as the case may be.

11. In the case of the promotion of a pawn, the actual pawn move is indicated, followed immediately by the first letter of the new piece. Examples: d8Q, f8N, b1B, g1R.

Essential Abbreviations

O—O	= castling with rook h1 or rook h8 (king-side castling)
O—O—O	= castling with rook a1 or rook a8 (queen-side castling)
x	= captures*
+	= check
++	= mate
e.p.	= captures "en passant"

Sample Game

1 d4 Nf6 2 c4 e6 3 Nc3 Bb4 4 Bd2 O—O 5 e4 d5 6 exd5 exd5 7 cxd5 Bxc3 8 Bxc3 Nxd5 9 Nf3 b6 10 Qb3 Nxc3 11 bxc3 c5 12 Be2 cxd4 13 Nxd4 Re8 14 O—O Nd7 15 a4 Nc5 16 Qb4 Bb7 17 a5 bxa5, etc.

Other Systems
Recognized Until January 1, 1981

---

* There is a' variation in the indication of a capture which is used by a number of chess players, consisting in the use of a colon (:) instead of an *x.* From January 1, 1981 on, this variation will no longer be recognized in the interest of uniformity and clarity.

Algebraic System: Long Form

1. Each move in the long form is indicated by (a) the first letter of the piece in question, (b) the square of departure, and (c) the square of arrival. Pawns are not indicated by their first letter, but are recognized by the absence of such a letter. The squares of departure and of arrival are joined by a hyphen. Examples: Bd4-e5, Ng1-f3, Ra1-d1, e4-e5, d2-d4.
2. When a piece or pawn makes a capture, the hyphen is replaced by an *x*. Examples: Bd4xe5, Ng1xf3, Ra1xd1, e4xf5, d2xe3.

Sample Game

1 d2-d4 Ng8-f6 2 c2-c4 e7-e6 3 Nb1-c3 Bf8-b4 4 Bc1-d2 O-O 5 e2-e4 d7-d5 6 e4xd5 e6xd5 7 c4xd5 Bb4xc3 8 Bd2xc3 Nf6xd5 9 Ng1-f3 b7-b6 10 Qd1-b3 Nd5xc3 11 b2xc3 c7-c5 12 Bf1-e2 c5xd4 13 Nf3xd4 Rf8-e8 14 O-O Nb8-d7 15 a2-a4 Nd7-c5 16 Qb3-b4 Bc8-b7 17 a4-a5 b6xa5, etc.

Descriptive System

1. Each piece and pawn is indicated by the first letter, a capital letter, of its name. The pieces on the queen's side of the board in the initial position are indicated by a Q preceding to distinguish them from the similar pieces on the king's side of the board in the initial position, indicated by a K preceding. Examples: R, N, B, QR, KN.
2. For the first letter of the name of a piece, each player is free to use the first letter of the name which is commonly used in his country. Examples: F = fou (French for bishop), L = loper (Dutch for bishop).
3. The eight files (from left to right for White and from right to left for Black) are indicated by the pieces which occupy them in their initial position: *QR, QN, QB, Q, K, KB, KN,* and *KR,* respectively.

4. The eight ranks (each player counting from bottom to top from his side) are indicated by *1, 2, 3, 4, 5, 6, 7,* and *8,* respectively. Consequently, in the initial position the white pieces and pawns are placed on the first and second ranks, the black pieces and pawns on the seventh and eighth ranks from White's side and vice versa from Black's side.

5. As a consequence of the preceding rules, each of the sixty-four squares is indicated by two combinations of letters and numbers, depending upon whether White's or Black's move is being recorded.

Black

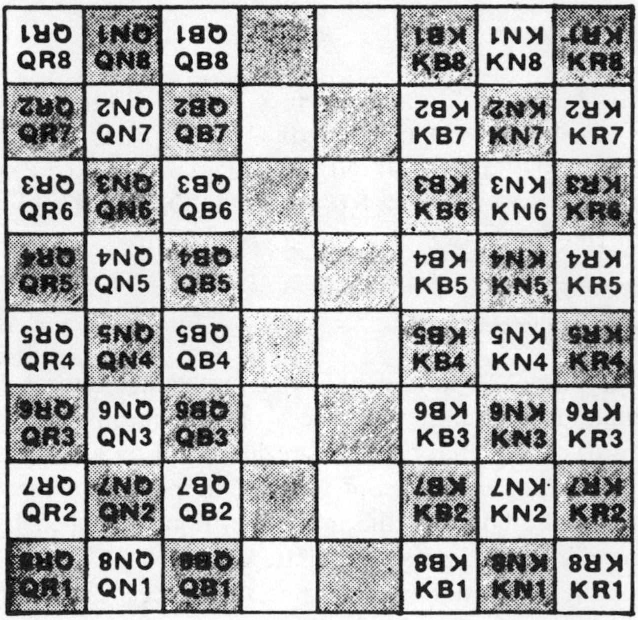

(Each square is labeled with two notations: the upside-down Black notation over the upright White notation, shown below as Black/White.)

QR1/QR8	QN1/QN8	QB1/QB8			KB1/KB8	KN1/KN8	KR1/KR8
QR2/QR7	QN2/QN7	QB2/QB7			KB2/KB7	KN2/KN7	KR2/KR7
QR3/QR6	QN3/QN6	QB3/QB6			KB3/KB6	KN3/KN6	KR3/KR6
QR4/QR5	QN4/QN5	QB4/QB5			KB4/KB5	KN4/KN5	KR4/KR5
QR5/QR4	QN5/QN4	QB5/QB4			KB5/KB4	KN5/KN4	KR5/KR4
QR6/QR3	QN6/QN3	QB6/QB3			KB6/KB3	KN6/KN3	KR6/KR3
QR7/QR2	QN7/QN2	QB7/QB2			KB7/KB2	KN7/KN2	KR7/KR2
QR8/QR1	QN8/QN1	QB8/QB1			KB8/KB1	KN8/KN1	KR8/KR1

White

6. Each pawn is indicated by the file on which it stands: QRP, QNP, QBP, QP, KP, KBP, KNP, and KRP.

7. A move to a vacant square is indicated by (a) the first letter(s) of the piece or pawn in question and (b) the

square of arrival, joined by a hyphen. When a move is written down, the basic forms R, N, B, and P (additionally, in the case of a pawn, the semi-condensed forms RP, NP, and BP) are used when only one piece or pawn of the specified type can move as indicated or if a recorded check identifies the move or capture. Examples: R—N3, B—B5, P—B4ch.

8. A capture is indicated by the first letter of the capturing and captured pieces or pawns, joined by an *x*. Examples: BxB, QxR, PxP, PxBP.

9. When a basic form would be ambiguous at any point in the indicated move,

(1) a king-side or queen-side piece or pawn is specified if the piece or pawn can easily be so identified;

(2) the basic form is used, followed by a virgule (/) and the rank (preferably) or the file on which the piece or pawn stands, whichever will unambiguously identify the piece or pawn.

Examples: (1) There are two knights, on the squares KN1 and Q2, and one of them moves to the square KB3: either KN—B3 or QN—B3, as the case may be.

(2) There are two knights, on the squares KN5 and KN1, and one of them moves to the square KB3: either N/5—B3 or N/1—B3, as the case may be.

If a capture takes place on the square KB3, the previous examples are changed by the substitution of an *x* for the hyphen and of the first letter of the captured piece or pawn for the square on which the capture takes place: (1) either KNxR or QNxR, (2) either N/5xR or N/1xR, as the case may be.

10. In the case of the promotion of a pawn, the actual pawn move is indicated, followed by a virgule and the first letter of the new piece. Example: PxR/Q.

N.B. In a slightly different form of the descriptive system used in non-English-speaking countries, the rank precedes the square of arrival without a hyphen. Examples (in Spanish): P4AD, C3AR, P4D.

Essential Abbreviations

O—O	=	castling with the king's rook
O—O—O	=	castling with the queen's rook
x	=	captures
ch	=	check (or, in Spanish, +)
e.p.	=	captures "en passant"

Sample Game

1 P-Q4 N-KB3 2 P-QB4 P-K3 3 N-QB3 B-N5 4 B-Q2 O-O
5 P-K4 P-Q4 6 KPxP PxP 7 PxP BxN 8 BxB NxP 9 N-B3
P-QN3 10 Q-N3 NxB 11 PxN P-QB4 12 B-K2 PxP 13 NxP
R-K1 14 O-O N-Q2 15 P-QR4 N-B4 16 Q-N4 B-N2 17 P-QR5
PxP, etc.

SUPPLEMENT NO. 2.

A. CORRESPONDENCE NOTATION

1. Each square of the chessboard is designated by a two-digit number as shown in the diagram below:

Black

8	18	28	38	48	58	68	78	88
7	17	27	37	47	57	67	77	87
6	16	26	36	46	56	66	76	86
5	15	25	35	45	55	65	75	85
4	14	24	34	44	54	64	74	84
3	13	23	33	43	53	63	73	83
2	12	22	32	42	52	62	72	82
1	11	21	31	41	51	61	71	81
	1	2	3	4	5	6	7	8

White

2. A move (including a capture) is indicated by stating the number of the square of departure and the number of the square of arrival, thus forming one four-figure number. Castling is expressed simply as a king's move. Thus, e2—e4 = 5254, and O—O = 5171 (king-side castling for White) or 5878 (king-side castling for Black).*

* The international method of recording pawn promotion is as follows. The first two digits denote the square of departure, the third digit denotes the

B. TELECOMMUNICATIONS NOTATION (UEDEMANN CODE)

1. Each square of the chessboard is designated by two letters as shown in the diagram below:

Black

MA	NA	PA	RA	SA	TA	WA	ZA
ME	NE	PE	RE	SE	TE	WE	ZE
MI	NI	PI	RI	SI	TI	WI	ZI
MO	NO	PO	RO	SO	TO	WO	ZO
BO	CO	DO	FO	GO	HO	KO	LO
BI	CI	DI	FI	GI	HI	KI	LI
BE	CE	DE	FE	GE	HE	KE	LE
BA	CA	DA	FA	GA	HA	KA	LA

White

2. A move (including a capture) is indicated by stating the two letters of the square of departure and the two letters of the square of arrival, thus forming one group of four letters. Castling is expressed simply as a king's move. Thus, e4 = GEGO and O—O = GAKA (king-side castling for White) or SAWA (king-side castling for Black).

---

file of arrival, and the fourth digit indicates the type of piece selected for promotion, using 1 for a queen, 2 for a rook, 3 for a bishop, and 4 for a knight. For example, if a pawn moves from square 37 to square 38 and is promoted to a queen, the move is written 3731; if Black moves a pawn from 62 to 61 and promotes a knight, the move is written 6264.

SUPPLEMENT NO. 3. RULES FOR PLAYING CHESS BETWEEN SIGHTED AND BLIND PLAYERS

In competitive chess between sighted and blind players, the use of two chessboards shall be obligatory, the sighted player using a normal chessboard, while the blind player uses one with securing apertures.

The following regulations shall govern play:

1. The moves shall be announced clearly, repeated by the opponent, and executed on his board.

2. On the blind player's board, a piece shall be deemed "touched" when it has been taken out of the securing aperture.

3. A move shall be deemed executed when—
    (a) a piece is placed into a securing aperture;
    (b) in the case of a capture, the captured piece has been removed from the board of the player who has the move; and
    (c) the move has been announced.

Only after this shall the opponent's clock be started.

4. A chess clock with flag, made specially for the blind, shall be admissible.

5. The blind player may keep the score of the game in braille or on a tape recorder.

6. A slip of the tongue in announcing a move must be corrected immediately and before starting the clock of the opponent.

7. If, during a game, different positions should arise on the two boards, such differences have to be corrected with the assistance of the arbiter and by consulting both players' game scores. In resolving such differences, the player who has written down the correct move, but executed the wrong one, has to accept certain disadvantages.

8. If, when such discrepancies occur, the two game scores are also found to differ, the moves shall be retraced up to the point where the two scores agree, and the arbiter shall readjust the clocks accordingly.

9. The blind player shall have the right to make use of an assistant who shall have the following duties:

(a) to make the moves of the blind player on the board of the opponent;

(b) to announce the moves of the sighted player;

(c) to keep the score for the blind player and start his opponent's clock;

(d) to inform the blind player, at his request, of the number of moves made and the time consumed by both players;

(e) to claim the game in cases where the time-limit has been exceeded; and

(f) to carry out the necessary formalities in cases where the game is adjourned.

10. If the blind player does not require any assistance, the sighted player may make use of an assistant who shall announce the sighted player's moves and make the blind player's moves on the sighted player's board.

RULES FOR FIVE-MINUTE LIGHTNING CHESS

To be applied in FIDE-tournaments and strongly recommended to be used in all other international five-minute lightning tournaments.

Duration of the Game

1. Each player must make all his moves within five minutes on his clock.

The Clock

2. All the clocks must have a special device, usually a "flag," marking the end of the time-control period.

3. Before play begins the players should inspect the position

of the pieces and the setting of the clock. If they have omitted to do this, no claim shall be accepted after each player has made his first move.

4. Each player must handle the clock with the same hand with which he handles his pieces. Exception: It is permitted to perform the castling move by using both hands.

5. The arbiter should stipulate at the beginning of the tournament the direction the clocks are to face, and the player with the black pieces decides on which side of the board he will sit.

6. No player is permitted to cover more or less permanently the button of his own clock with one of his fingers.

7. During the game the clock must not be picked up by either player.

The Won Game

8. A game is won by the player—
   (a) who has mated his opponent's king;
   (b) whose opponent declares that he resigns;
   (c) whose opponent completes an illegal move, which includes leaving his king in check or moving his king into check, but only if the player claims the win before he himself touches a piece (see Rule No. 18) or captures that king as valid proof;
   (d) whose opponent's flag falls first, at any time before the game is otherwise ended.

9. A player must claim a win himself by immediately stopping both clocks and notifying the arbiter. To claim a win under Rule No. 8d, the player's flag must be up and his opponent's flag must be down after the clocks have been stopped. If both flags are down, the game is declared a draw (see Rule No. 10c).

The Drawn Game

10. A game is drawn—
    (a) if one of the kings is stalemated;

(b) by agreement between the players during the game, not before or after the game;

(c) if the flag of one player falls after the flag of the other player has already fallen and a win has not been claimed;

(d) if a player demonstrates a perpetual check or a forced repetition of position under the conditions of Article 18.2 of the Laws of Chess;

(e) if both players have insufficient material for a possible checkmate (only king vs. king, king and bishop vs. king, king and knight vs. king, king and bishop vs. king and bishop on diagonals of the same color); or

(f) if one player has insufficient material for a possible checkmate as described in Rule No. 10e and his opponent's flag falls first.

11. The player having the white pieces must notify the arbiter of a drawn game.

Miscellaneous

12. If a player accidentally displaces one or more pieces, he must replace them on his own. If it is necessary, his opponent may start the player's clock without making a move in order to make sure that the player replaces the displaced pieces on his own time.

13. Play shall be governed by the FIDE Laws and the FIDE Interpretations of the Laws, in all cases to which they apply and in which they are not inconsistent with these rules. In particular, Article 8 ("The Touched Piece") remains in full force.

    If a player first touches one piece and then moves another, his opponent should restart the player's clock, if it is necessary, and inform him that he must complete the move in accordance with Article 8.

14. In case of a dispute, either player may stop the clocks while the arbiter is being summoned. All of these rules are sub-

ject to interpretation by the arbiter, whose decisions are final.

15. Spectators and participants are not to speak or otherwise to interfere in another game. If a spectator interferes in any way, such as by calling attention to a flag-fall or an illegal move, the arbiter may cancel the game and rule that a new game be played in its stead, as well as expel the offending party from the playing rooms. The arbiter, too, must refrain from calling attention to a flag-fall or an illegal move, as this is entirely the responsibility of the players themselves.

16. The arbiter shall not handle the clock except in the case of a dispute or when both players ask him to do so.

17. A move is completed as soon as the player's hand has released a piece in accordance with Article 7 of the Laws of Chess.

18. Illegal moves unnoticed by both players cannot be corrected afterwards, nor can they afterwards lead to a claim of a won game under Rule No. 8c.

19. Before a five-minute lightning tournament, the organizers should hand out a copy of these rules to each participant, or, if this is not possible, see that a sufficient number of copies of these rules are posted in the playing room at least half an hour before the tournament is to begin.

USCF SECTION

Preface to the USCF Section

Pairing Rules of the United States Chess Federation

Suggested Rules for Play Involving Computational Machinery

Summary of Important Rules for USCF Tournament Players

Major Changes from the 1974 Edition

General Information on the United States Chess Federation

Preface to the USCF Section

As tournament chess develops, the USCF has an obligation to keep pace by working to standardize clear and consistent rules, first to provide the competitors with information about the terms under which they will be playing and to assure them of a substantially uniform application of the rules throughout the United States, and second to furnish USCF Certified Tournament Directors with guidance on how to perform their responsibilities correctly.

The USCF Tournament Rules, as currently amended, have been placed, for convenience of reference, together with the FIDE Laws and Interpretations in the FIDE Section of this book. The current USCF Pairing Rules, perfected in some cases by comments and experience since the publication of the 1974 version, are included in this section, as approved by the USCF.

As improvements are continuously being considered and new publications in the field of tournament direction are projected, the comments of directors and players alike are welcomed. Such comments may be addressed to the editor, Martin E. Morrison, at the U.S. Chess Federation, who will be happy to receive them.

Pairing Rules of the
United States Chess Federation*

Purpose

The purpose of these Pairing Rules is to standardize the conduct of Swiss-System and round-robin tournaments for USCF rating. Since even the practices of the best tournament directors vary, specific variations are provided in certain cases. Moreover, there must be legitimate flexibility to deal with the particular requirements of individual tournaments and to take advantage of experimentation for the improvement of the pairing rules. Therefore, other variations of the basic system are allowed, but only when announcement is made in advance of the first round.

Variations

The director may choose to use any of the variations listed in the following rules or variations other than those listed (if he feels they are in accord with the goals of these Pairing Rules), *but only if written and also, whenever possible, oral announcement is made in advance of the first round.*

---

* See also the FIDE Interpretations of Article 21 of the Laws of Chess for relevant material.

A. RATINGS-CONTROLLED INDIVIDUAL SWISS-SYSTEM TOURNAMENTS

Introduction

The Swiss System permits a relatively large number of players to take part in a relatively short tournament. The Swiss System is frequently used in large weekend tournaments, in which a hundred or more players can participate in one tournament of, e.g., four or five rounds. It is also used in longer tournaments extending over one or two weeks with several hundred players and, e.g., ten to thirteen rounds. A higher ratio of rounds to players will bring about more accurate results, and where a particularly large field is anticipated, several sections (such as expert, amateur, and beginner) can be run simultaneously.

The purpose of the Swiss System is to produce a clear winner in as few rounds as possible; therefore, in pairing, the system consistently works to reduce the number of players with perfect or high scores. The fundamental laws of the Swiss System are that in each round players with the same score must play each other whenever possible and that no contestant may play the same opponent more than once.

In the first round, all the entrants have equal scores of zero and play together in one group. Then, in the second round, the players are divided into three groups: (a) the first-round winners, (b) the players who drew their games, and (c) the first-round losers. The players in each group are paired.

The same system of grouping is continued throughout the tournament. Thus, in the fourth round, those who tallied 3–0 in the first three rounds are paired, those who scored 2½–½ are paired, etc., down to the group that scored 0–3 (see Rule No. 6 on Scoring).

The round-robin tournament is undoubtedly the best kind of competition when nearly all the contestants have similar ratings. Nothing can match the round robin for an all-master tournament, but a ratings-controlled Swiss-System tournament is a more effective and fairer type of competition than any other when there is a wide range of playing strength among the contestants and when there are more players than can be handled in a single round robin of reasonable duration. Thus, although it is only an imperfect approximation of the round robin, the Swiss System has practical advantages for large tournaments which outweigh the variables introduced by the system in the pairings.

Pairing Cards

1. A pairing card is made out for each entrant on which the director records for each round the color of the player's pieces, the opponent's (name and) pairing number, the player's score in the game, and the player's cumulative tournament score (see Rule No. 6).

Ratings of Players

2. The rating entered on a player's card is his last-published USCF rating (unless use of a given Rating List was specified in the advance publicity). A foreign entrant without a USCF rating may be given his most recent FIDE international rating, or, if he has none, his national rating.* Entrants without any official ratings may be given estimated ratings based on whatever information the director wishes to use.

Pairing Numbers

3. After the entry list is closed, all the cards are arranged in the order of the players' ratings, the cards of entrants without even estimated ratings being placed at the bottom.

VARIATION. Unrated players, for their actual strength to be reflected more accurately in the pairings, may be arranged—

* Chess Federation of Canada ratings can be used without change. British Chess Federation ratings can be converted to FIDE international rating units by multiplying by 8, then adding 600. Ingo ratings can be converted to FIDE international rating units by subtracting 8 times the Ingo rating from 2,840.

(a) just below the average rating of the tournament or section, or

(b) approximately one-fifth of the way up from the bottom.

Players with identical ratings and players without even estimated ratings are arranged by lot. Then the pairing numbers of all players are entered on the pairing cards, starting with the highest-rated player as No. 1. These pairing numbers generally remain unchanged throughout the tournament.

Late Entrants

4. The director may accept and pair entries after the announced closing time, but a late entrant defaults any round he has missed for which it is inconvenient or too late for the director to pair the entrant for play. The director may also assign a "pairing score," to be used only for the purpose of pairing the entrant, if the director feels that pairing each defaulted game as a loss would be unfair to the other players.

The pairing numbers of late entrants follow in sequence the last number assigned before the entry list was closed, but, in pairing, late entrants are arranged in the order described in Rule No. 3 regardless of their pairing numbers.

Byes

5. If the total number of players in any round of a tournament or section of a tournament is uneven, one player is given a bye. A player must not be given a bye more than once, nor is a bye to be given simply because a player enters late. In the first round the bye is given to the player with the lowest last-published USCF rating, in subsequent rounds to the lowest-ranked eligible officially-rated player, rank in this case being determined first by score, then by official rating (estimated ratings should not be used for awarding byes). If all players eligible for the bye are without official ratings, the bye is awarded by lot.

Scoring

6. The scoring is one point for a win, one-half point for each player for a draw, zero for a loss. A bye is scored as one point for the byed player. Any game defaulted because of a player's failure to appear within one hour after the starting time (FIDE Article 17.2) is scored as one point for the winner and zero for the loser, and the defaulting player is not paired for the succeeding rounds without an excuse acceptable to the director. Defaulted games (as those of a late entrant or of a player who is excused from being paired in a round after the director has been notified in advance that the player will be unable to play) are scored as zero. The remaining games of a player who is excused, withdrawn because of a default without notice, or expelled from the tournament are scored as zero. The scores of unplayed games are circled on the pairing cards and wallchart.* Each player's final position is determined by the total of his score.

VARIATION. A bye may be scored as one-half point for the byed player.

Unfinished Games

7. A game that is not finished before it is time to pair the next round is temporarily scored as a draw for pairing purposes. When an unfinished game is completed, the correct results and cumulative scores are entered on the players' cards.

VARIATION. A game that is not finished before it is time to pair the next round may be temporarily adjudicated for pairing purposes. Written and also, whenever possible, oral announcement must be made in advance of the first round of the exact procedures to be used. In making an adjudica-

---

* All games played in USCF-rated events (with or without clocks) are rated, including games decided by time forfeit, games decided when a player fails to appear for resumption after adjournment, and games played by a player who subsequently withdrew or was not permitted to continue. Games in which the opponent made no move (defaulted games) are considered as unplayed and are not rated.

tion, the director should seek out the best advice that is available to him and should give proper weight to the degree of objectivity of that advice. The objective of the adjudication is to predict the probable result of the unfinished game. Therefore, the adjudication should give primary consideration to the position existing on the board, though such additional factors as the respective strengths of the players and the times remaining on their clocks may be considered as well, according to the adjudication procedures announced for the tournament. The players themselves may not be required to declare their evaluation of or objectives in the game or be penalized for refusing to do so.

Basic Swiss-System Laws

8. All Pairing Rules are subject to the following basic Swiss-System laws.

  (a) A player must not be paired with any other player more than once.
  (b) Players with equal scores must be paired if it is possible to do so.
  (c) If it is impossible to pair all players with equal scores, every player who is not paired with an opponent whose score is the same as his own must be paired with an opponent whose score is as close to his own as possible.

Pairing the First Round (See also Rule No. 23)

9. After the bye, if any, is given, the pairing cards are arranged in the order described in Rule No. 3 and are divided into two equal groups. The players in the top half are paired in consecutive order with those in the bottom half. For example, if there are forty players, No. 1 is paired with No. 21, No. 2 with No. 22, etc.

VARIATION. If specifically requested by the players involved, minor transpositions may be made in the first two rounds of a tournament at the director's discretion in order to avoid pairing players from the same region, city, club, team, family, etc., *but only to the extent that the results of the tournament as a whole are not substantially affected by this procedure.*

Pairing Subsequent Rounds (See also Rule No. 23)

Score Groups and Rank

10. In these rules the expression "score group," or simply "group," is used in reference to a group of players having the same score. Sometimes a group may consist of only one player whose score is unequaled by any other player.

Individual "rank" is determined first by score, then by rating, in the order described in Rule No. 3.

Order of Pairing Groups

11. In general, the order of pairing is from the group with the highest score down to the group with the lowest score. Occasionally, in the late rounds, the pairing of the lower-score groups may have to be adjusted to conform to the basic Swiss-System laws (Rule No. 8), if many of the players in those groups have met before.

Method of Pairing Each Score Group

12. In the second and as many of the subsequent rounds as possible, the players are paired as follows.

   (a) Any odd men removed from the next higher score group are paired first as described in Rule Nos. 13–15.
   (b) Within each score group, after the odd man, if any, has been removed, the cards of the remaining players are arranged in the order described in Rule No. 3 and divided into two equal sections. The players in the top half (with the higher ratings) are paired with those in the bottom half (with the lower ratings) in as close to consecutive order as possible. *Transpositions* in the

bottom half of a group are made to make the pairings conform to the basic Swiss-System laws (Rule No. 8) and to give as many players as possible their due colors (Rule Nos. 19–21). If it is impossible to meet the two requirements just mentioned, *interchanges* between the top half and the bottom half may be made, but not simply to preserve alternation of colors. Every effort must be made, however, to observe the principle of pairing the higher-rated against the lower-rated players in as close to consecutive order as possible [but see Rule No. 21—Variation]. *Note:* Directors differ somewhat in their exact methods for implementing this procedure, but any reasonable method, followed consistently, is acceptable.

Rules on Odd Men

13. If there is an odd number of players in a score group, the lowest-ranked player is ordinarily treated as the odd man. However, the pairings in the group must accord with the basic Swiss-System laws (Rule No. 8).

In removing an odd man to the next-lower group, the prime consideration is that the remaining players in the original group can all be paired with each other. If the lowest-ranked player in the odd-numbered group has already played all the players in the next-lower group, the next lowest-ranked player is treated as the odd man and paired with the highest-ranked player he has not met in the next-lower group. This procedure is followed until a player in the odd-numbered group is found who has not played all the players in the next-lower group.

If all the players in an odd-numbered group have played all the players in the next-lower group, the lowest-ranked player in the odd-numbered group is treated as the odd man and paired with the highest-ranked player he has not met in the second-lower group. In all cases, when an odd man is removed from a score group, there must be a possible pairing of all the players remaining in the original group. Sometimes two players who have met in a previous round must be treated as odd men because there is no possible way in which either of them can be paired in their original group.

Method of Pairing One Odd Man

14. The odd man is paired with the highest-ranked player he has not met in the next-lower group.

VARIATION 1. The odd man may be paired with the highest-ranked player whom he has not met in the next-lower group and who is due the opposite color.

VARIATION 2. Except in the last quarter of a tournament, a player should not be treated as an odd man or paired with an odd man more than once unless such a pairing cannot be avoided. To implement this variation, an indication should be made on the card of a player who has been treated as an odd man or paired with an odd man. In the last quarter of a tournament, a player may be treated as an odd man or paired with an odd man as many times as necessary.

Method of Pairing More Than One Odd Man

15. If there are two odd men to be paired, the order in which they are paired is determined by their rank according to Rule No. 10. If both cannot be paired, rank determines which is paired and which is removed to another group.

Pairing Players with Unfinished Games

16. Players with unfinished games (Rule No. 7) should not usually be treated as odd men if it is possible to avoid doing so.

Color Allocation

General Principles

17. The director assigns colors to all players. His primary objective in a tournament with an even number of rounds is to give white and black the same number of times to as many

players as possible, and, in a tournament with an odd number of rounds, to give white and black the same number of times to every player, plus one extra white or black. After the first round the director attempts to give as many players as possible their due colors, round by round (Rule Nos. 19–21).

First-Round Colors

18. In the first round, when the top half of the ranked field plays the bottom half, the color assigned to all the odd-numbered players in the top half is chosen by lot, and the opposite color is given to all the even-numbered players in the top half. Opposite colors are assigned to the opponents in the bottom half of the field as the pairings are made. (Once the first-round colors are thus chosen by lot, Rule Nos. 19–21 preserve equitable color allocation, and no further lots are necessary.)

Due Colors in Succeeding Rounds

19. As many players as possible are given their due colors, as described in Rule Nos. 20–21, so long as the pairings conform to the basic Swiss-System laws (Rule No. 8). Equalization of colors takes priority over alternation of colors.

Equalization of Colors

20. As many players as possible are given the color that equalizes the number of times they have played as White and Black. When it is necessary to pair any two players who are due to be given the same equalizing color, the higher-ranked player has priority in getting the equalizing color, whether white or black.

Alternation of Colors

21. After colors have been equalized in a round, as many players as possible should be given, in the next round, the color opposite to that which each received in the preceding round, the purpose being to continue alternation of colors. When it is

necessary to pair any two players who are due to be given the same alternating color, the higher-ranked player has priority in getting the alternating color, whether white or black. However, a player should not be assigned the same color three times in a row. Transpositions, but not interchanges (see Rule No. 12b), may be made to preserve alternation of colors.

VARIATION 1. Neither transpositions nor interchanges should be made simply to preserve alternation of colors. If both players are due for the same color, the higher-ranked player has priority in getting his due color, whether white or black.

VARIATION 2. In the last round of a tournament with an odd number of rounds, when two players who have had an equal number of whites and blacks are paired, or in the last round of a tournament with an even number of rounds, when it is necessary to pair two players who are due the same equalizing color, the director may allow such players to choose colors by lot. If one of the players is absent when the round begins, his clock is started, and the lot is taken upon his arrival.

Color for Unplayed Games

22. Unplayed games (including byed games) do not count for color.

Accelerated Methods of Pairing Early Rounds (Variations)

23. In a tournament where the players-to-rounds ratio exceeds the optimum (16:4, 32:5, 64:6, etc.), the chances of producing a clear winner are decreased. Since the effect of these variations decreases sharply when the players are of approximately the same playing strength (as in a tournament divided into sections by playing strength), this variation should be used only when there is a wide disparity in playing strength overall.

VARIATION 1. The following method produces more drawn games and makes it less likely that two contestants will finish with perfect scores.

In the first round, after the bye, if any, is issued and the pairing cards are arranged in the order described in Rule No. 3, the cards are divided into *four* sections, and the first quarter of the field is paired against the second quarter, then the third quarter against the fourth quarter.

In the second and possibly later rounds, if the number of players with perfect scores exceeds the optimum for the number of rounds remaining, the cards of the players with perfect scores are arranged in the order described in Rule No. 3, and the first quarter is paired against the second quarter, the third quarter against the fourth quarter. The cards of the players in the score group just below are arranged and paired similarly. Players in the other score groups are paired according to the basic system.

VARIATION 2. The following method results in only about half as many players having a perfect score as under the basic system and increases the opportunity of a single winner.

In the first round, after the bye, if any, is issued, the pairing cards are arranged in the order described in Rule No. 3. Then the field is divided from top to bottom into four groups (A, B, C, D) as close to the same size as possible and paired as follows:

(a) In one section, the players in group A are paired against the players in group B in consecutive order.

(b) In a second section, the players in group C are paired against the players in group D in consecutive order. In each section, colors are assigned according to Rule No. 18.

For the second-round pairings, the players are regrouped as follows:

A: winners from section (a);

B: remaining players from section (a), adding 100 points to the ratings of the players who drew;

C: winners and players who drew from section (b), subtracting 100 points to the ratings of the players who drew;

D: remaining players from section (b).

All groups are arranged in the order described in Rule No. 3. Group A is divided in half and paired. Group B is paired with group C. (If there are more players in group B than in group C, the extra players are added to the top of group D. If there are more players in group C than in group B, the extra players are paired with the top players in group D.) Group D is divided in half and paired.

In each second-round group, odd men are treated, colors are allocated, and players are paired as in the basic system.

For the third and all subsequent rounds of the tournament, the rating points added are removed and the pairings made as in the basic system.

B. RATINGS-CONTROLLED TEAM SWISS-SYSTEM TOURNAMENTS

Basic Rules

1. Most of the rules for Ratings-Controlled Individual Swiss-System Tournaments apply to teams in Swiss-System tournaments. Some rules are modified as indicated below.

Pairing Cards

2. A card similar to that used for Individual Swiss Tournaments is used, but provision is made for match scores and game points.

Order of Boards

3. Team members should be placed in board order according to ratings, and they must play in that order throughout the tournament. The highest-rated player is Board No. 1, etc. Unrated players may play on any board as long as their position reflects their actual strength in relation to the rated players. The director may authorize in advance of the tournament that players may be placed out of rating order within a specific point limit, such as 25 or 50 points.

Alternate team members are used according to whatever system is announced in advance.

Team Ratings

4. The rating entered on a team's card is the average of the ratings of the regular team members. In the case of unrated players:

(a) If a top or bottom board is unrated, the rating assigned is 50 points (or some other announced number of points) from that of the player on the next board.

(b) If a middle board is unrated, the rating assigned is averaged from the ratings of the next higher- and lower-rated players.

Pairing Rules

5. Teams are paired and ranked first by their match scores, then by their ratings.

Color Allocation

6. In each team the colors given to the individual players alternate from Board No. 1 down. If the player at Board No. 1 has white, then No. 2 has black, No. 3 has white, etc. Rule Nos. 17–22 for Individual Swiss-System Tournaments are applicable to team tournaments, but in each rule the colors referred to are those of the player at Board No. 1.

Scoring

7. Each member of a team scores game points as described in Rule No. 6 for Individual Swiss-System Tournaments. A team scores one match point for a win against another team, one-half match point for a draw, zero for a loss, on the basis of game points greater than, equal to, or less than the opposing team, respectively. A team's match score for a bye is one point. Any round defaulted because of a team's failure to appear within one hour after the starting time is scored as one point for the winning team and zero for the losing team, and the defaulting team is

not paired for the succeeding rounds without an excuse acceptable to the director. Defaulted rounds (as those of a late-entering team or of a team which is excused from being paired in a round after the director has been notified in advance that it will be unable to play) are scored as zero. The remaining games of a team which is excused, withdrawn because of a default without notice, or expelled from the tournament are scored as zero. The scores of unplayed games (rounds) are circled on the pairing cards and wallchart. Each team's final position is determined by the total of the match points scored by the team.

C. INDIVIDUAL ROUND-ROBIN TOURNAMENTS

Basic Rules

1. Each player plays one game with each of the other players. In a double round robin he plays each of the other players twice, once with white and once with black.

Pairing

2. After being divided into sections (e.g., by similar rating), if any, players are assigned numbers by lot within their sections. The pairings, order of rounds, and color allocation in each game are shown in the International Tables of Rounds (see Appendix III). The player with the first number of each pairing has the white pieces. If there is an odd number of players, the last even number in the applicable table is assigned to the bye. For a double round robin the applicable table is used to pair the players for play in the first part of the tournament in the manner described above. For the second part the same table is used, but the colors are reversed.

ROSLYN HIGH SCHOOL LIBRARY
Roslyn Heights, New York

38808

Scoring

3. The scoring is one point for a win, one-half point for each player for a draw, zero for a loss. Byes are not scored. Any game defaulted because of a player's failure to appear within one hour after the starting time (FIDE Article 17.2) is scored as one point for the winner and zero for the loser, and the defaulting player is withdrawn if without an excuse acceptable to the director. Defaulted games are scored as one point for the paired opponent and zero for the player. (See FIDE Interpretations Art. 21 [1970, 1973], Consequences When a Player or a Team Withdraws or Is Expelled from a Tournament, for scoring the remaining games of a player who is excused, withdrawn because of a default without notice, or expelled from the tournament.) The scores of unplayed games are circled on the wall chart. Each player's final position is determined by the total of his score.

D. TEAM ROUND-ROBIN TOURNAMENTS

Basic Rules

1. Rule No. 1 for Individual Round-Robin Tournaments applies to the teams.

Order of Boards

2. Rule No. 3 for Team Swiss-System Tournaments applies.

Pairing

3. Rule No. 2 for Individual Round-Robin Tournaments applies to the teams.

In each team the colors given to the individual players alternate from Board No. 1 down. If the player at Board No. 1 has white, then No. 2 has black, No. 3 has white, etc. In Rule No. 2 for Individual Round-Robin Tournaments, the colors referred to are those of the player at Board No. 1.

Scoring

4. Each member of a team scores game points as described in Rule No. 3 for Individual Round-Robin Tournaments. A team scores one match point for a win against another team, one-half match point for a draw, zero for a loss, on the basis of game points greater than, equal to, or less than the opposing team, respectively. Byes are not scored. Any round defaulted because of a team's failure to appear within one hour after the starting time is scored as one point for the winning team and zero for the losing team, and the defaulting team is withdrawn if without an excuse acceptable to the director. Defaulted rounds are scored as one point for the paired opposing team and zero for the team itself. (See FIDE Interpretations Art. 21 [1970, 1973], Consequences When a Player or a Team Withdraws or Is Expelled from a Tournament, for scoring the remaining games of a team which is excused, withdrawn because of a default without notice, or expelled from the tournament.) The scores of unplayed games (rounds) are circled on the wallchart. Each team's final position is determined by the total of the match points scored by the team.

Appendix I*

PRIZES

Announcement of Prizes

1. In pre-tournament publicity, the prizes to be awarded and the methods to be used in allocating the announced prizes must be stated.

Awarding Prizes

2. Unless other methods are stated in pre-tournament publicity, the director should abide by the following guidelines in allocating prizes.†

---

* Appendices I and II apply equally when a team is concerned instead of a player.

† *Example 1*

Player U:	5–0	1st:	$400	Player U wins $200
Player V:	5–0	2nd:	$200	Player V wins $200
Player W:	5–0	1st A:	$100	Player W wins $200
Player X:	4½–½	1st B:	$ 50	Player X wins $ 0
Player Y: (Class A)	4½–½			Player Y wins $100
Player Z: (Class B)	4½–½			Player Z wins $ 50

Example 2

Player T:	5–0	1st:	$250	Player T wins $225
Player U:	5–0	2nd:	$200	Player U wins $225
Player V:	4½–½	3rd:	$150	Player V wins $100
Player W: (Class A)	4½–½	4th:	$100	Player W wins $100
		1st A:	$ 75	
Player X: (Class A)	4½–½	2nd A:	$ 50	Player X wins $100
		1st B:	$ 75	
Player Y: (Class B)	4½–½			Player Y wins $100
Player Z: (Class A)	4–1			Player Z wins $ 50

(a) Cash Prizes.

(1) No winner should receive more than one cash award for which he is eligible. The award may be one full cash prize (if he is a clear winner) or parts of two or more cash prizes (if he wins tied with others). Such special prizes as "upset" or "best game" may be excepted from this rule.

(2) A clear winner of more than one cash prize should be awarded the greatest prize.

(3) Tied winners of place prizes, or tied winners (in the same class) of class prizes, should be awarded all the cash prizes involved, summed and divided equally, but no more than one cash prize (in order of amount) should go into the division for each winner.

(4) If winners of class prizes tie with winners of place prizes, all the cash prizes involved should be summed and divided equally among the tied winners, no more than one cash prize, in order of amount, to go into the division for each winner, unless the class-prize winners would receive more cash by dividing only the class prizes.

(5) An announced class prize must be awarded even if only one player in that class completes his schedule of play.

(b) Non-cash (Indivisible) Prizes.

(1) Irrespective of any cash award won, no winner should receive more than one non-cash prize, the most valuable to which he is entitled.

(2) Although tie-breaking should be avoided if possible, ties may be broken to award trophies or merchandise, to determine which player wins any title at stake or qualifies for another contest, or to serve any other purpose than the award of cash prizes.

Example 3

Player X:	5–0	1st:	$100	Player X wins $100
Player Y:	4½–½	2nd:	$ 75	Player Y wins $ 75
(Class A)		1st A: $50 & clock		& clock
Player Z:	4–1			Player Z wins $ 50
(Class A)				

(3) Two players tieing for a championship are considered co-champions; the tie may be broken if more than two players tie for a championship.

Questionable Cases

3. The director is the final authority on the distribution of prizes in complex or questionable cases. Any player who fails to complete his schedule of play without an excuse acceptable to the director relinquishes any prizes to which he would otherwise be entitled.

Appendix II

TIE-BREAKING

Methods to Be Used

1. Although tie-breaking should be avoided if possible, in those cases when tie-breaking must be used, such as to award a single trophy, the following methods are to be used unless written, and also, whenever possible, oral announcement is made in advance of the first round. The director is the final authority on breaking ties in cases unresolved by these methods.

Swiss-System Tournaments

2. *Cumulative System.* For each player in the tie is found the sum of his cumulative tournament scores after each round. (For example, if a player scores a win in round one, losses in rounds two through four, and a draw in round five, the sum of his cumulative tournament scores after each round—1, 1, 1, 1, 1½—is 5½.) One point is subtracted from the sum for each unplayed win or one-point bye.

Round-Robin Tournaments

3. *Partial-Score System* (also known as Sonneborn-Berger System). For each player in the tie is found the sum of the final scores of all the opponents he has defeated, together with half the final scores of all the opponents with whom he has drawn (nothing is added for games he has lost or for unplayed games).

If the tie still remains, the results of the games between the players involved in the tie are used.

Appendix III

INTERNATIONAL TABLES OF ROUNDS

Table A
3 or 4 Players

Round	Pairings	
1	1:4	2:3
2	4:3	1:2
3	2:4	3:1

TABLE B
5 or 6 Players

Round	Pairings		
1	1:6	2:5	3:4
2	6:4	5:3	1:2
3	2:6	3:1	4:5
4	6:5	1:4	2:3
5	3:6	4:2	5:1

TABLE C—7 or 8 Players

Round	Pairings			
1	1:8	2:7	3:6	4:5
2	8:5	6:4	7:3	1:2
3	2:8	3:1	4:7	5:6
4	8:6	7:5	1:4	2:3
5	3:8	4:2	5:1	6:7
6	8:7	1:6	2:5	3:4
7	4:8	5:3	6:2	7:1

Table D—9 or 10 Players

Round	Pairings				
1	1:10	2:9	3:8	4:7	5:6
2	10:6	7:5	8:4	9:3	1:2
3	2:10	3:1	4:9	5:8	6:7
4	10:7	8:6	9:5	1:4	2:3
5	3:10	4:2	5:1	6:9	7:8
6	10:8	9:7	1:6	2:5	3:4
7	4:10	5:3	6:2	7:1	8:9
8	10:9	1:8	2:7	3:6	4:5
9	5:10	6:4	7:3	8:2	9:1

TABLE E—11 or 12 Players

Round	Pairings					
1	1:12	2:11	3:10	4:9	5:8	6:7
2	12:7	8:6	9:5	10:4	11:3	1:2
3	2:12	3:1	4:11	5:10	6:9	7:8
4	12:8	9:7	10:6	11:5	1:4	2:3
5	3:12	4:2	5:1	6:11	7:10	8:9
6	12:9	10:8	11:7	1:6	2:5	3:4
7	4:12	5:3	6:2	7.1	8:11	9:10
8	12:10	11:9	1:8	2:7	3:6	4:5
9	5:12	6:4	7:3	8:2	9:1	10:11
10	12:11	1:10	2:9	3:8	4:7	5:6
11	6:12	7:5	8:4	9:3	10:2	11:1

TABLE F—13 or 14 Players

Round	Pairings						
1	1:14	2:13	3:12	4:11	5:10	6:9	7:8
2	14:8	9:7	10:6	11:5	12:4	13:3	1:2
3	2:14	3:1	4:13	5:12	6:11	7:10	8:9
4	14:9	10:8	11:7	12:6	13:5	1:4	2:3
5	3:14	4:2	5:1	6:13	7:12	8:11	9:10
6	14:10	11:9	12:8	13:7	1:6	2:5	3:4
7	4:14	5:3	6:2	7:1	8:13	9:12	10:11
8	14:11	12:10	13:9	1:8	2:7	3:6	4:5
9	5:14	6:4	7:3	8:2	9:1	10:13	11:12
10	14:12	13:11	1:10	2:9	3:8	4:7	5:6
11	6:14	7:5	8:4	9:3	10:2	11:1	12:13
12	14:13	1:12	2:11	3:10	4:9	5:8	6:7
13	7:14	8:6	9:5	10:4	11:3	12:2	13:1

TABLE G—15 or 16 Players

Round				Pairings				
1	1:16	2:15	3:14	4:13	5:12	6:11	7:10	8:9
2	16:9	10:8	11:7	12:6	13:5	14:4	15:3	1:2
3	2:16	3:1	4:15	5:14	6:13	7:12	8:11	9:10
4	16:10	11:9	12:8	13:7	14:6	15:5	1:4	2:3
5	3:16	4:2	5:1	6:15	7:14	8:13	9:12	10:11
6	16:11	12:10	13:9	14:8	15:7	1:6	2:5	3:4
7	4:16	5:3	6:2	7:1	8:15	9:14	10:13	11:12
8	16:12	13:11	14:10	15:9	1:8	2:7	3:6	4:5
9	5:16	6:4	7:3	8:2	9:1	10:15	11:14	12:13
10	16:13	14:12	15:11	1:10	2:9	3:8	4:7	5.6
11	6:16	7:5	8:4	9:3	10:2	11:1	12:15	13:14
12	16:14	15:13	1:12	2:11	3:10	4:9	5:8	6:7
13	7:16	8:6	9:5	10:4	11:3	12:2	13:1	14:15
14	16:15	1:14	2:13	3:12	4:11	5:10	6:9	7:8
15	8:16	9:7	10:6	11:5	12:4	13:3	14:2	15:1

TABLE H—17 or 18 Players

Round				Pairings					
1	1:18	2:17	3:16	4:15	5:14	6:13	7:12	8:11	9:10
2	18:10	11:9	12:8	13:7	14:6	15:5	16:4	17:3	1:2
3	2:18	3:1	4:17	5:16	6:15	7:14	8:13	9:12	10:11
4	18:11	12:10	13:9	14:8	15:7	16:6	17:5	1:4	2:3
5	3:18	4:2	5:1	6:17	7:16	8:15	9:14	10:13	11:12
6	18:12	13:11	14:10	15:9	16:8	17:7	1:6	2:5	3:4
7	4:18	5:3	6:2	7:1	8:17	9:16	10:15	11:14	12:13
8	18:13	14:12	15:11	16:10	17:9	1:8	2:7	3.6	4:5
9	5:18	6:4	7:3	8:2	9:1	10:17	11:16	12:15	13:14
10	18:14	15:13	16:12	17:11	1:10	2:9	3:8	4:7	5:6
11	6:18	7:5	8:4	9:3	10:2	11:1	12:17	13:16	14:15
12	18:15	16:14	17:13	1:12	2:11	3:10	4:9	5:8	6:7
13	7:18	8:6	9:5	10:4	11:3	12:2	13:1	14:17	15:16
14	18:16	17:15	1:14	2:13	3:12	4:11	5:10	6:9	7:8
15	8:18	9:7	10:6	11:5	12:4	13:3	14:2	15:1	16:17
16	18:17	1:16	2:15	3:14	4:13	5:12	6:11	7:10	8:9
17	9:18	10:8	11:7	12:6	13:5	14:4	15:3	16:2	17:1

TABLE I—19 or 20 Players

Round	Pairings									
1	1:20	2:19	3:18	4:17	5:16	6:15	7:14	8:13	9:12	10:11
2	20:11	12:10	13:9	14:8	15:7	16:6	17:5	18:4	19:3	1:2
3	2:20	3:1	4:19	5:18	6:17	7:16	8:15	9:14	10:13	11:12
4	20:12	13:11	14:10	15:9	16:8	17:7	18:6	19:5	1:4	2:3
5	3:20	4:2	5:1	6:19	7:18	8:17	9:16	10:15	11:14	12:13
6	20:13	14:12	15:11	16:10	17:9	18:8	19:7	1:6	2:5	3:4
7	4:20	5:3	6:2	7:1	8:19	9:18	10:17	11:16	12:15	13:14
8	20:14	15:13	16:12	17:11	18:10	19:9	1:8	2:7	3:6	4:5
9	5:20	6:4	7:3	8:2	9:1	10:19	11:18	12:17	13:16	14:15
10	20:15	16:14	17:13	18:12	19:11	1:10	2:9	3:8	4:7	5:6
11	6:20	7:5	8:4	9:3	10:2	11:1	12:19	13:18	14:17	15:16
12	20:16	17:15	18:14	19:13	1:12	2:11	3:10	4:9	5:8	6:7
13	7:20	8:6	9:5	10:4	11.3	12:2	13:1	14:19	15:18	16:17
14	20:17	18:16	19:15	1:14	2:13	3:12	4:11	5:10	6:9	7:8
15	8:20	9:7	10:6	11:5	12:4	13:3	14:2	15:1	16:19	17:18
16	20:18	19:17	1:16	2:15	3:14	4:13	5:12	6:11	7:10	8:9
17	9:20	10:8	11:7	12:6	13:5	14:4	15:3	16:2	17:1	18:19
18	20:19	1:18	2:17	3:16	4:15	5:14	6:13	7:12	8:11	9:10
19	10:20	11:9	12:8	13:7	14:6	15:5	16:4	17:3	18:2	19:1

TABLE J—21 or 22 Players

Round	Pairings										
1	1:22	2:21	3:20	4:19	5:18	6:17	7:16	8:15	9:14	10:13	11:12
2	22:12	13:11	14:10	15:9	16:8	17:7	18:6	19:5	20:4	21:3	1:2
3	2:22	3:1	4:21	5:20	6:19	7:18	8:17	9:16	10:15	11:14	12:13
4	22:13	14:12	15:11	16:10	17:9	18:8	19:7	20:6	21:5	1:4	2:3
5	3:22	4:2	5:1	6:21	7:20	8:19	9:18	10:17	11:16	12:15	13:14
6	22:14	15:13	16:12	17:11	18:10	19:9	20:8	21:7	1:6	2:5	3:4
7	4:22	5:3	6:2	7:1	8:21	9:20	10:19	11:18	12:17	13:16	14:15
8	22:15	16:14	17:13	18:12	19:11	20:10	21:9	1:8	2:7	3:6	4:5
9	5:22	6:4	7:3	8:2	9:1	10:21	11:20	12:19	13:18	14:17	15:16
10	22:16	17:15	18:14	19:13	20:12	21:11	1:10	2:9	3:8	4:7	5:6
11	6:22	7:5	8:4	9:3	10:2	11:1	12:21	13:20	14:19	15:18	16:17
12	22:17	18:16	19:15	20:14	21:13	1:12	2:11	3:10	4:9	5:8	6:7
13	7:22	8:6	9:5	10:4	11:3	12:2	13:1	14:21	15:20	16:19	17:18
14	22:18	19:17	20:16	21:15	1:14	2:13	3:12	4:11	5:10	6:9	7:8
15	8:22	9:7	10:6	11:5	12:4	13:3	14:2	15:1	16:21	17:20	18:19
16	22:19	20:18	21:17	1:16	2:15	3:14	4:13	5:12	6:11	7:10	8:9
17	9:22	10:8	11:7	12:6	13:5	14:4	15:3	16:2	17:1	18:21	19:20
18	22:20	21:19	1:18	2:17	3:16	4:15	5:14	6:13	7:12	8:11	9:10
19	10:22	11:9	12:8	13:7	14:6	15:5	16:4	17:3	18:2	19:1	20:21
20	22:21	1:20	2:19	3:18	4:17	5:16	6:15	7:14	8:13	9:12	10:11
21	11:22	12:10	13:9	14:8	15:7	16:6	17:5	18:4	19:3	20:2	21:1

TABLE K—23 or 24 Players

Round	Pairings											
1	1:24	2:23	3:22	4:21	5:20	6:19	7:18	8:17	9:16	10:15	11:14	12:13
2	24:13	14:12	15:11	16:10	17:9	18:8	19:7	20:6	21:5	22:4	23:3	1:2
3	2:24	3:1	4:23	5:22	6:21	7:20	8:19	9:18	10:17	11:16	12:15	13:14
4	24:14	15:13	16:12	17:11	18:10	19:9	20:8	21:7	22:6	23:5	1:4	2:3
5	3:24	4:2	5:1	6:23	7:22	8:21	9:20	10:19	11:18	12:17	13:16	14:15
6	24:15	16:14	17:13	18:12	19:11	20:10	21:9	22:8	23:7	1:6	2:5	3:4
7	4:24	5:3	6:2	7:1	8:23	9:22	10:21	11:20	12:19	13:18	14:17	15:16
8	24:16	17:15	18:14	19:13	20:12	21:11	22:10	23:9	1:8	2:7	3:6	4:5
9	5:24	6:4	7:3	8:2	9:1	10:23	11:22	12:21	13:20	14:19	15:18	16:17
10	24:17	18:16	19:15	20:14	21:13	22:12	23:11	1:10	2:9	3:8	4:7	5:6
11	6:24	7:5	8:4	9:3	10:2	11:1	12:23	13:22	14:21	15:20	16:19	17:18
12	24:18	19:17	20:16	21:15	22:14	23:13	1:12	2:11	3:10	4:9	5:8	6:7
13	7:24	8:6	9:5	10:4	11:3	12:2	13:1	14:23	15:22	16:21	17:20	18:19
14	24:19	20:18	21:17	22:16	23:15	1:14	2:13	3:12	4:11	5:10	6:9	7:8
15	8:24	9:7	10:6	11:5	12:4	13:3	14:2	15:1	16:23	17:22	18:21	19:20
16	24:20	21:19	22:18	23:17	1:16	2:15	3:14	4:13	5:12	6:11	7:10	8:9
17	9:24	10:8	11:7	12:6	13:5	14:4	15:3	16:2	17:1	18:23	19:22	20:21
18	24:21	22:20	23:19	1:18	2:17	3:16	4:15	5:14	6:13	7:12	8:11	9:10
19	10:24	11:9	12:8	13:7	14:6	15:5	16:4	17:3	18:2	19:1	20:23	21:22
20	24:22	23:21	1:20	2:19	3:18	4:17	5:16	6:15	7:14	8:13	9:12	10:11
21	11:24	12:10	13:9	14:8	15:7	16:6	17:5	18:4	19:3	20:2	21:1	22:23
22	24:23	1:22	2:21	3:20	4:19	5:18	6:17	7:16	8:15	9:14	10:13	11:12
23	12:24	13:11	14:10	15:9	16:8	17:7	18:6	19:5	20:4	21:3	22:2	23:1

Suggested Rules for Play
Involving Computational Machinery

The following rules are suggested for use in USCF-rated tournaments when one or both players is a computer. In matters not covered by these rules, play is governed by the FIDE Laws, by the FIDE Interpretations of the Laws, and by the USCF Tournament rules and Pairing Rules, interpreted by the arbiter. In such games the "player" shall be considered to be the chess algorithm being executed on a specific computer.

The following regulations shall govern play:

1. For the algorithmic player (computer), a piece shall be deemed "touched" when a move involving that piece is communicated.

2. A move shall be deemed executed when the move has been executed on the playing chessboard. Only after this shall the opponent's clock be started.

3. The computer and/or the operator shall keep the score of the game.

4. If, during a game, different positions should arise on the playing chessboard and on the chessboard or representation thereof maintained by the algorithmic player, such differences shall be corrected with the assistance of the arbiter by consulting both players' game scores. In resolving such differences, the player whose score has the correct move, but who has executed a wrong one, has to accept certain disadvantages.

5. If, when such discrepancies occur, the game scores are also found to differ, the moves shall be retraced up to the point where the scores agree, and the arbiter shall readjust the clocks accordingly.

6. The algorithmic player's operator(s) shall have the following duties:

    (a) to make the moves of the algorithmic player on the playing chessboard;

(b) to communicate the moves of the opponent to the algorithmic player;

(c) to operate the chess clock for the algorithmic player;

(d) to inform the algorithmic player, at its request, of the time consumed by either or both players;

(e) to claim the game in cases where the time-limit has been exceeded;

(f) to carry out the necessary formalities in cases where the game is adjourned;

(g) to communicate proposals of a draw between the algorithmic player and the opponent;

(h) to carry out the functions associated with machine or communication failure. During restart, program parameters must be reset to the most recent values. Board position and status, along with clock time, may also be entered.

7. The opponent may appoint a deputy to record the game score.

8. Communication to and from the algorithmic player regarding the moves of the game shall be made in a standard (clear and unambiguous) notation.

9. During the course of a game, an algorithmic player may not request additional data or information which requires human intervention. Such a request shall be considered a violation of Article 19.1a of the Laws.

10. With the approval of the arbiter in advance of the first round, the operator may resign or accept a draw on the behalf of the algorithmic player.

Summary of Important Rules for USCF Tournament Players

The topics and references indicated below constitute a basic set of rules with which every tournament player should be thoroughly familiar. However, any participant in a USCF-rated tournament is assumed to be familiar with *all* the rules and contracts to abide by them whenever he enters a rated event.

Tournament Equipment	FIDE Interpretations Art. 21 (1957, 1975)
Castling	Article 6.1
Touched Piece	Article 8
Draw by Repetition of Position	Articles 12.3 and 18.2
Recording of Games	Articles 13.1 and 13.2
Reporting of Results	USCF Tournament Rule Art. 13.1 (3)
Setting and Starting the Chess Clock	USCF Tournament Rule Art. 14.3 (1) and 14.3 (4)
Adjournment of the Game	Article 15.1
Loss on Time	Article 17.1
Defaults Without Notice	USCF Tournament Rule Art. 17.2 (1)
Proposal of a Draw	Article 18.1
Premature Draws, Thrown Games	Article 18.1
Conduct of the Players	Article 19
Appeals	USCF Tournament Rule Art. 20.3 (1–7)
Penalties	USCF Tournament Rule Art. 20.4 (1)

Major Changes from the 1974 Edition

End of the Game	FIDE Interpretation Art. 11.1 (1976), FIDE Interpretation Art. 14.4 (1976)
Rate of Play	USCF Tournament Rule Art. 14.1 (1)
Accumulated Time	USCF Tournament Rule Art. 14.1 (2)
Time-Forfeits	USCF Tournament Rule Art. 17.1 (1–6)
Sealed Moves	FIDE Interpretation Art. 17.3 (1976)
Draws by Repetition	FIDE Interpretation Art. 18.2 (1976)
Team Competitions	FIDE Interpretation Art. 19.1a (1976B)

General Information on the United States Chess Federation

186 Rt. 9W
New Windsor, N.Y. 12550

MEMBERSHIP

Anyone interested in advancing United States chess is eligible for membership, with benefits which include—

(1) a subscription to *Chess Life & Review,* the monthly magazine which is an official publication of the USCF (except participating Junior and Spouse Members);

(2) a national chess rating, based on performances in USCF-rated tournaments, for which membership is a requirement of entry, and (except Participating Junior and Spouse Members) monthly notification of that rating on the magazine mailing label;

(3) the opportunity to compete in Official USCF Postal Chess Tournaments, for which membership is a requirement of entry, and receipt of the special insert in *Chess Life & Review* which is sent only to participants in these tournaments; and

(4) discounts on chess books and equipment from the USCF's Catalog of Chess Books and Equipment by convenient mail-order.

Regular Membership: $15.00 (one year), $28.50 (two years), $40.00 (three years).

Junior Membership (under 19 years of age at the new date of expiration, if a resident of the U.S. or Canada or submitting a membership through a USCF affiliate): $8.00 (one year), $15.00 (two years), $21.50 (three years).

Participating Junior Membership (same age and residency requirements as for a Junior Membership, with exceptions in benefits noted above): $2.50 per year.

Senior Membership (if passed their 65th birthday): $10.00 per year.

Spouse Membership (spouses of Regular, Life, or Sustaining Members—spouse's USCF Identification Number must be supplied—with exceptions in benefits noted above): $10.00 per year.

Special Membership (spouses of Regular, Life, or Sustaining Members—spouse's USCF Identification Number must be supplied—with exceptions in benefits noted above): $10.00 per year.

Special Membership (for the blind): $3.50 per year.

Institutional Subscription: $15.00 per year.

AFFILIATION

Any organization of chess players may affiliate with the USCF, with benefits which include—

(1) the privilege of sponsoring USCF-rated tournaments in accordance with USCF procedures for conducting and reporting rated tournaments and under the supervision of a Certified Tournament Director;

(2) free listing of rated tournaments in the "Tournament Life" department of *Chess Life & Review;*

(3) the privileges of sponsoring Non-Rated Beginners' Tournaments and of listing these in *Chess Life & Review;*

(4) being entitled to a commission on individual membership dues collected and forwarded to the USCF;

(5) discounts on merchandise from the USCF's Catalog of Chess Books and Equipment by convenient mail order;

(6) a subscription to *Chess Life & Review;*

(7) receipt of the USCF Rating List Supplement.

Regular Affiliation: $25.00 per year.

College Chess Club Affiliation: $15.00 per year.

High School Chess Club Affiliation: $10.00 per year.

Prison Chess Club Affiliation: $10.00 per year.

Affiliates are not agents of the USCF for any purpose.

TOURNAMENT DIRECTOR CERTIFICATION

Any USCF member may become a Certified Tournament Director by filling out an application form, available from the USCF National Office, passing a written, open-book (multiple-choice) at-home examination which tests his knowledge of the *Official Rules of Chess* and the USCF forms and procedures for conducting rated tournaments.

Tournaments to be rated by the USCF for the National Rating List must be supervised by a Certified Tournament Director at the appropriate level.

Certified Tournament Directors are not agents of the USCF for any purpose.

OFFICIAL USCF POSTAL CHESS TOURNAMENTS

Any USCF member has the opportunity to compete in Official USCF Postal Chess Tournaments. The USCF conducts, on an ongoing basis, the following three postal tournaments:

(1) *Class Tournaments.* Four-man tournaments at minimum expense in entry fee ($4.00) and postage (two games on one

set of postcards). Each player has six games, one as White, one as Black, with each of three opponents.

(2) *Victory Tournaments.* Seven-man tournaments reserved exclusively for those with two completed assignments and no forfeit losses. Each player has six games, White against three opponents, Black against three. Entry fee is $7.50. A credit of $25.00 is awarded to the first-place winner in each tournament for purchases of chess books and equipment from the USCF Catalog.

(3) *US Open Postal Chess Championship (Golden Knights).* Seven-man qualification tournaments with classes mixed; successful competitors progress to the finals. Top scorers win substantial cash prizes, all who complete play in the finals win Golden Knights pins, and all others who complete their assignments win a discount coupon for purchases of chess books and equipment from the USCF Catalog.

In Class and Victory Tournaments, entries are strictly by class. In Victory Tournaments, only players with already established USCF postal ratings are admitted.

Postal tournament entrants must send to the USCF National Office the proper entry fee, full name, USCF Identification Number, address, type of tournament, class, and whether the entrant is a previous USCF postal chess entrant or a newcomer (in which case a suitable class should be selected).

All games in USCF Postal Chess Tournaments are rated in a national postal chess rating system, which is totally separate from the over-the-board rating system. The basic purpose of the ratings is to assure equitable matching of players in Class and Victory Tournaments. A player is started with 600 as his initial rating if he enters as a new player or below average (Class D); 900 as average (Class C); 1200 as above average (Class B); or 1300 as well above average (Class A).

In addition to the three on-going tournaments listed above, the USCF is currently organizing new varieties of postal-chess competition, including an Absolute Postal Class Championship and Postal Chess Class Championships, which will be announced in *CL&R* when sections are being formed.

Expanded Table of Contents